MODERN TEA

Modern TEA

A Fresh Look at an Ancient Beverage

LISA BOALT RICHARDSON

PHOTOGRAPHS BY JENIFER ALTMAN

CHRONICLE BOOKS

SAN FRANCISCO

Photograph on page 23 and text copyright © 2014 by Lisa Boalt Richardson.

Library of Congress Cataloging-in-Publication Data available.
ISBN 978-1-4521-1229-9

Manufactured in China

Designed by Alice Chau & Agnes Lee
Photographs by Jenifer Altman

10 9 8 7 6 5 4 3 2 1

Chronicle Books LLC
680 Second Street
San Francisco, California 94107
www.chroniclebooks.com

*To Joe, my husband and tea partner for life,
and to our children, Zach and Kate, the perfect
pairing to complete our family.*

Introduction

9

CHAPTER ONE

WHAT IS TEA?

Where It's Grown and How It Becomes Specialty Tea

11

CHAPTER TWO

THE ART OF TEA

Buying, Storing, Steeping, and Tasting

49

CHAPTER THREE

TEA CEREMONIES AND RITUALS

Experiencing Tea in Many Different Ways

81

CHAPTER FOUR

BEYOND THE CUP

Pairing, Cooking, Cocktails, and More

113

CHAPTER FIVE

THE BUZZ ABOUT TEA

Caffeine, Health, Coffee, and Sustainability

137

Resources

156

Select Bibliography

158

Index

160

Acknowledgments

164

INTRODUCTION

My fascination with tea began one day years ago with a great cup of black cinnamon-spiced raspberry tea. My thirst was quenched right away, but I remained intrigued about what I had just imbibed and yearned to know more about this brilliance in a cup. That made me even more intent on finding out as much as I could about tea. I started reading, researching, and attending conferences, all of which eventually led to the birth of my speaking, educating, writing, and consulting tea business in 2000.

Maybe your interest in tea began with a great cup, too, and now you also thirst to know more about this ancient beverage, second only to water in popularity around the world. Or perhaps tea is like an old acquaintance whom you realize you don't know much about and think you should know more. This book is a culmination of questions I have asked and answers I discovered as I explored this complex beverage in classrooms and libraries, tea shops and tearooms, tea fields and tea factories.

In the following pages, I hope to present tea in a fresh and interesting way. First, you will learn the history of tea around the world and how teas, all of which come from the same plant, become different colors. Then you will discover how to buy, store, steep, and taste tea for its many

different nuances. You might have wondered if tea is grown sustainably and how tea farmers are caring for the environment. I tackle these topics as well, along with explaining which tea is the healthiest to drink and whether you should worry about how much caffeine it contains. I also explain how the beverage is celebrated through diverse ceremonies and rituals around the world and encourage you to re-create them in your own home. Finally, you will find out how to use tea beyond the cup, from pairing it with food and cooking with it to adding it to cocktails, compost piles, beauty lotions, and more.

Although I am considered a tea specialist, and some may even call me an expert, my education about this beverage never ends. I continue to read about tea, travel to countries where it is grown, and drink it with the same eagerness I felt when I started my tea journey. For me, tea is much more than a beverage. It is a lifestyle that I will continue to pursue, and I hope you will as well. Happy sipping!

CHAPTER ONE

WHAT IS TEA?

Where It's Grown and How It Becomes Specialty Tea

Tea is a beverage, a commodity, a ceremony, an afternoon tradition, a drink of peace, a pick-me-up, a path to meditation, and much more. It comes from a sturdy evergreen bush that thrives in warm, wet places, and age-old prescriptions rule how the meticulously plucked fresh leaves of the plant are processed to produce what you steep in a teapot. Tea has a long, rich history as well, one laden with both fanciful legends and hard facts. Part of the enjoyment of drinking tea is learning as much as you can about everything from its botanical lineage and centuries-old history to the differences between black tea and green tea, oolong tea and dark tea.

WHAT IS TEA?

Of the many legends about how tea was discovered, probably the most popular one names the Chinese emperor Shennong (sometimes spelled Shen Nung), known as the father of Chinese agriculture, as the first person to steep tea and drink the steaming brew. The year was 2737 B.C., and while the emperor was boiling water to purify it, a gust of wind carried a scattering of tea leaves from a nearby wild bush into his kettle. Instead of trying to retrieve and discard the leaves, he decided to infuse them, and then sat back and enjoyed the resulting beverage. There is no written record of this first cup, however. Indeed, no references to tea appear in any Chinese literature until some three millennia later. But regardless of whether the story of Shennong and the inadvertent cup of tea is myth or truth, we do know that the tea plant likely originated in the southwestern Chinese province of Yunnan, where its leaves were initially appreciated for their medicinal qualities.

In time, much of the rest of the world developed a taste for the combination created when those wayward leaves serendipitously blew into the emperor's kettle of boiling water. The bush that yielded them was the *Camellia sinensis* plant, and by definition the six classes, or types, of true tea recognized today—white, green, yellow, black, oolong, and dark—must come from this particular species of tropical and subtropical evergreen native to Asia.

You may be familiar with the camellia plant, as many different species are grown around the globe. They are known for their beautiful, shiny, deep green leaves and stunning flowers in a variety of colors. *C. sinensis* produces a small white blossom with a yellow center that is not as showy as the blooms of many of its cousins. But tea growers are not seduced by the beauty of the flowers in any case. In fact, they discourage the plants from blossoming because they know that all the plant's energy must go into producing leaves that will yield fine teas.

The genus name *Camellia* comes from the latinized form of the surname of Georg Josef Kamel (sometimes spelled Camel; 1661–1706), a Czech-born Jesuit missionary who became a well-known botanist in his time. He didn't discover the plant, nor did he name it, though he did tend tea bushes in gardens in the Philippines. Carl Linnaeus, creator of the taxonomy system still in use today, chose to pay tribute to Kamel's contributions to botany by using his name for the genus, one of many in the Theaceae family. The word *sinensis* is Latin for "from China."

C. sinensis boasts two main varieties: *C. sinensis* var. *sinensis* and *C. sinensis* var. *assamica*. The former botanical name, though it seems

Herbal Infusions

Many herbs, flowers, dried fruits, and even barks and pine needles can be infused—that is, steeped in water (or other liquid) to extract their soluble elements—to make a lovely brew. These beverages are properly called herbal infusions or tisanes but never teas.

Among the best-known infusions are mint, chamomile, and hibiscus. A nutty-flavored, burnt-red infusion made from the needlelike leaves of the rooibos bush is arguably the most fashionable tisane at the moment. The plant is native to South Africa, where the beverage, commonly known as bush tea or red tea, has long been hailed as an antidote to everything from asthma to eczema. A tisane made from tulsi, also known as holy basil, is currently popular as well. The plant originates in Asia, and in India, drinking an infusion made from its leaves is believed to reduce stress and ensure longevity.

Nearly all infusions are caffeine-free. Among the popular exceptions is yerba maté, which is consumed in Argentina, Uruguay, and parts of Brazil.

repetitive, simply indicates that the plant is the Chinese variety of the species. The name of the latter variety specifies it is from Assam, in northeastern India, close to the Himalayas. *C. sinensis* var. *sinensis* tends to have a smaller leaf and can withstand colder temperatures than its counterpart. It can grow upward of 15 ft/4.5 m if left untouched. The larger-leaved Indian variety, which can reach 40 ft/12.2 m in the wild, is hardy but cannot tolerate frost.

Researchers work tirelessly to come up with new *C. sinensis* cultivars; that is, plants that are created or selected for their desired characteristics, such as improved disease resistance or the ability to withstand drought or other severe weather conditions, and some five hundred cultivars have been recorded to date. Any class of tea can be produced from any of these cultivars, though it might not be the best in its category. But every hot, comforting, flavorful beverage you sip that is dubbed *tea* is properly named only if it comes from the *C. sinensis* plant. If it doesn't, it is more correctly referred to as an herbal infusion or a tisane (see "Herbal Infusions," left).

Tea fields are generally called tea estates, tea gardens, or tea plantations, depending on where they are located in the world, and may be flat land, rocky terraced terrain, rolling hills, or steep mountainsides. The plants are typically kept at a height of 3 to 4 ft/1 to 1.2 m to make them easier to harvest and are regularly pruned to stimulate growth and fullness.

WHERE IS TEA GROWN?

Tea has long been traditionally grown in just five countries—China, Japan, India, Sri Lanka, and Taiwan—and today they remain the source of the finest teas in the world. China, as already noted, is likely the birthplace of tea, and its people were responsible for developing the techniques used for processing the six classes of tea we have today. It is also the only country that currently produces all six classes, being the sole purveyor of dark tea. Dark teas are distinctly different from the other classes because they undergo a postproduction secondary fermentation process. Tea cultivation and processing has spread from these Asian countries to some forty countries around the world, where *C. sinensis* is grown for both the specialty market (see page 19, "What Is Specialty Tea?") and to satisfy the large commodity demand for tea bags.

Some sources indicate that tea may have been cultivated in Japan as early as the Nara period (A.D. 710–794), but those dates cannot be verified. Documents do show that seeds of the tea plant were carried to Japan in 805, during the Heian period, by Buddhist monks Saichō and Kūkai, who, as members of a diplomatic mission organized by the Japanese emperor, had gone to China to further their study of Buddhist doctrine. Soon after the monks' return, the emperor encouraged the cultivation of tea, which at first was drunk only by royalty and priests. In time, its consumption spread to the samurai class, the gentry, and then finally, by the seventeenth century, to the masses. Today, Japan is famous for its green teas but also produces some black teas. Its industry is unique in its approach to tea processing, which uses computerized automation, unlike China, where much of the work continues to rely on human judgment.

In the same century that the common people of Japan first enjoyed tea, Dutch ships began carrying tea from Japan and Indonesia to Amsterdam

My First Tea Plantation

The first tea field I ever visited was the Charleston Tea Plantation in South Carolina. I was attending a small conference of southern United States tea business owners in the fall of 2006, and the conference organizers were able to schedule a visit to the plantation before it opened to the public. I had never before been so close to the plant that produces the beverage that I had come to love, and the unique atmosphere of this Southern coastal plantation, with its lush evergreen bushes, moss-draped live oaks, and tropical Atlantic Ocean breezes, added to the experience. That and subsequent visits whetted my appetite to see tea fields in Asia.

and then on to ports in France and other European countries. (The Chinese were reluctant to welcome foreign ships in their ports, so the Dutch were forced to pick up their Chinese tea in Jakarta.) Tea first arrived in London in 1657, but it did not become a fashionable beverage until the royal marriage between Portugal's Catherine of Braganza and England's Charles II in 1662. Because the Chinese had granted the Portuguese trading privileges at the southern Chinese port of Macau in the 1550s, the Lisbon royals were already serious tea drinkers by the time Catherine's dowry, which included a number of tea chests, was delivered to London. She quickly made taking tea at court a common practice, and in time, all of England took up the new beverage.

As the popularity of tea steadily increased and trade relations with the Far East became strained, the British began to look to sources beyond China to supply their beloved beverage. By the mid-nineteenth century, they had established large tea plantations in two of their colonies, India and Ceylon (today's Sri Lanka). They discovered *C. sinensis* var. *assamica* growing wild in India but initially planted *C. sinensis* var. *sinensis*, believing that it was better to go with a plant that had produced great tea for centuries. The British also invented machinery that mimicked much of what was being done by hand in China, a development that revolutionized the industry. Although India and Sri Lanka are historically famous for their black teas, both

countries now also produce white, green, and a small amount of oolong.

Because of its proximity to China, Taiwan seems a natural candidate for tea growing, but it didn't happen quickly. It was only in the mid-1800s that tea was planted and processed for export. Today, Taiwan is renowned for its oolongs, sometimes referred to as Formosa oolongs, after Ilha Formosa (*formosa* means "beautiful"), the name the Portuguese gave the island in 1544. It also produces good black and green teas.

Tea cultivation spread from Asia to other parts of the globe, and today, Kenya is among the world's top exporters. You can also find tea grown on a varying scale everywhere from the Black Sea coast of Russia and the highlands of Rwanda to New Zealand, Australia, Ecuador, and Uganda. Surprisingly, it is also grown in very small amounts in the United States.

C. sinensis was taken to South Carolina around 1800 by François André Michaux, the royal botanist to Louis XVI of France. Along with other floral beauties, it was planted as an ornamental near Charleston at the Middleton Barony Plantation, now known as Middleton Place, the country's oldest landscaped garden. Beginning in the mid-1800s, tea farms were started in a few areas around the state, but all of them failed by 1907, sometimes because of the death of the owner and other times because of either costs or

A Pair of Taiwan Tea Gardens

In October 2010, I traveled to Taiwan with a group of tea enthusiasts to tour some of the country's world-famous tea gardens. There is a beauty to a tea field—the fresh air, the emerald-green lushness—that takes your breath away, and each garden we visited was distinctive, with the farmer's personal touch evident. Some gardens were on flat land and some were on high, verdant, mist-shrouded mountains. Two in particular stood out for me because of their splendor.

One was the Bagua Tea Garden (*bagua* is one of the primary analytical tools used in feng shui), in the mountainous Shanlinsi tea district. Mr. Lin, who runs the tea store connected with the garden, explained that the plants had been positioned according to the lay of the land, which resulted in a highly unusual—and breathtakingly beautiful—configuration of elaborate circular rows that extend far down the hillsides. As I sipped the garden's oolong tea in a little, white Eastern-style cup, complete with hand-painted blue fish swimming in the bottom, and looked out at the artistry of the rows and the majesty of the surrounding mountains, I knew it was a day I would never forget.

The second memorable stop was the Wang Ting Tea Garden, located near the town of Ruili, in the Alishan mountain range. Getting there was not easy, as the road was narrow, with lots of twists and turns and plenty of patches that were unpaved or had been washed away in a storm. As we ascended, I counted roughly three dozen switchbacks, and many times I closed my eyes when large trucks passed, as the embankment looked frighteningly

close. Although the trip was arduous, it was well worth it, for Wang Ting is perhaps my favorite tea garden to date.

The tea garden is owned and operated by Mr. Wong, who, at the age of eighteen, began to work alongside his father on the farm and eventually took it over when his father retired. The cottage farm and factory operation has slowly modernized to meet the demand for tea in the region, installing solar-powered transparent vinyl withering panels and updated rolling machines (see page 22, "Orthodox and Nonorthodox Production"). The factory was not nearly as impressive as the farm, however. It had been raining when we arrived, and as we left the processing facility behind and traveled even higher up the mountain, the rain stopped. When I stepped out of the van and into the tea garden, the emerald-green leaves of the *C. sinensis* bushes were shimmering and sparkling in the sunlight that was trying to push its way through the clouds. Some of the garden was flat and some was terraced against the rising hillsides. As I walked beside the rain-soaked bushes, I didn't mind getting wet, because it may have been the most glorious view I had ever seen. The heavy clouds and fog were so low that they seemed to touch the garden; it was as if the sky and the earth were one. Beyond the tea fields I could see a valley and a ring of mountains, both of them embraced by the billowy clouds. This place was new to me, yet somehow familiar, and I felt as if I was visiting a dear friend that I had not seen in a long time.

quarrels, or perhaps both. In the early 1960s, the Lipton tea company established an experimental farm on Wadmalaw Island in Charleston County, which it maintained for a quarter century. Ownership then shifted to two business partners, who named the farm the Charleston Tea Plantation and continued to grow high-quality tea until their partnership fell apart and the land moved to the auction block in 2003. Fortunately, the R. C. Bigelow tea company stepped in and saved the farm, and tea continues to be harvested there.

High-quality tea is also being grown on a very small scale in Skagit County, Washington, by the Japanese American Sakuma family, which has been farming in the area since the 1930s. And following several failed attempts to cultivate *C. sinensis* in Hawaii, one as early as the late 1880s, a cultivar that is happy in both the tropics and volcanic soil was developed early in the twenty-first century. Shortly after that, the University of Hawaii and the United States Department of Agriculture joined forces to study the feasibility of commercial production, and a plot of land was soon successfully under cultivation. Now, all of the tea in Hawaii is produced by individual farmers working mostly by hand. The yield is quite small, but the prices it commands are impressive.

The growing number of specialty tea drinkers in the United States is being matched by a rising interest in cultivating tea in the country. In 2013, the United States League of Tea Growers was started by Jason McDonald, who operates a tea farm in Mississippi. The newly formed association hopes to serve as an invaluable resource to North American tea farmers as they begin to cultivate their land. Only time will tell if tea grown and processed in North America will become important in the specialty tea market.

What may be even more surprising to some than finding tea growing in North America is what is happening in England. For centuries, the British demand for tea drove its cultivation in India, Sri Lanka, and Africa, but only recently has anyone thought of trying to nurture it in U.K. soil.

The owners of the Tregothnan Estate in Cornwall, which has been in the Boscawen family since 1335 and is also the seat of the Falmouth viscountship, took on this challenge. At an industry event in 2010, I met Jonathon Jones, the horticulturist who made the suggestion to grow *C. sinensis* on the estate. He shared with a group of tea experts how Lord and Lady Falmouth, who hired him as the head gardener in 1996, asked him what they could do on their land that would not only tie them to their rich history but also last for hundreds of years into the future. He researched the question thoroughly and realized that the camellias that grew wild at Tregothnan could be the answer. The English had never attempted to grow tea in England before, and it was always assumed that it couldn't be done. But Jones found that the estate's topography and climate were similar to that of India's famed Darjeeling tea region. His initial experiment did not produce much of a crop because strong winds damaged the plants. But the test did convince him that tea could be grown there successfully.

England's first homegrown tea was sold in 2005 to the legendary Fortnum & Mason, an English department store famous for its loose-leaf teas. The Boscawen family hopes to expand the amount of land under cultivation and would also like to open an international center dedicated to educating everyone about England's iconic cup. Although this small tea garden will never quench the thirst for tea in England, it does bring tea full circle to a citizenry who has made tea its beverage of choice.

WHAT IS SPECIALTY TEA?

Like specialty foods, specialty teas exemplify quality, innovation, and style due to their originality, authenticity, ethnic or cultural origin, ingredients, specific processing steps, limited supply, and/or distinctive use. Simply stated, specialty tea, sometimes referred to as fine

tea, is tea that is produced to have unique and exceptional qualities. Its leaves must be whole or nearly whole to reveal their distinctive flavor and characteristics, and they are sometimes blended or scented with other ingredients, such as citrus or smoke, to add appeal.

Specialty tea is never used for mass-market tea bags, which contain a blend of finely cut teas, known as commodity tea, to ensure a consistent flavor profile. There isn't anything wrong with commodity tea, but there isn't anything special about it either. It is blended to taste the same, year after year, to give consumers a consistency in their cup that they have come to expect.

Just as with fine wine, fine tea has a specific flavor profile that varies from year to year. And again like wine, it is known for its terroir, a term perhaps most used when discussing wine but also relevant to tea cultivation. In *The Oxford English Dictionary*, the word *terroir*, which comes from the Latin *terratorium*, literally "soil" or "land," is defined as "the complete natural environment in which a particular wine is produced, including factors such as the soil, topography, and climate." Simply put, it is the taste of the place where the wine—or the tea—originated. That means that specialty teas in the same classes will taste differently depending on where they are grown and processed. In other words, serious tea drinkers will know whether they are sipping a white tea from China or from Sri Lanka.

Two important aspects of the terroir of specialty tea are the season in which the leaves are harvested and the elevation at which the plants are grown. Darjeeling tea grown in the Himalayas, in northern India, is a good example of the factor of seasonality at work. The tea gardens, which boast rich, loamy soil, are dormant in winter, and new growth usually starts to sprout in mid-March. The harvest of these delicate, young new shoots is called the "first flush." It is followed by a second crop, known as the "second flush," which typically appears around mid-May and June. A fourth harvest, the "autumnal flush," is picked in the fall after the monsoon season. There is also a monsoon tea, or "third flush," that is harvested between July and September, but unlike the other flushes, it isn't nearly as popular a flush as the other ones mentioned. The first flush tastes remarkably floral, with hints of peach, honey, and a light muscatel note, and has good astringency. The infusion it makes is lighter in color than what you may expect from a black tea. The second flush is a bit more strongly flavored, has medium astringency, and carries more of the muscatel fruitiness that Darjeeling black teas are famous for. The color of the infusion is darker, more of an amber, but it still is not as dark as some black teas. The autumnal flush has a brisker flavor, is more full-bodied,

and has less of the floral or fruity muscatel notes than the first and second flushes. As you can see, tea grown in the same region brings a change in flavor to the cup depending on the season.

Likewise, tea cultivated in low elevations will not taste the same as those grown in high elevations, even within the same country. Using the example of Sri Lanka (Ceylon tea), the tea plantations range from slightly above sea level to well over 6,000 ft/1,800 m in elevation. The growing regions are divided into three categories: low-grown is from sea level to roughly 2,000 ft/600 m, mid-grown is from 2,000 to 4,000 ft/600 to 1,200 m, and high-grown is anything above 4,000 ft/1,200 m. Each category yields tea with its own unique characteristics.

Low-grown Ceylon teas deliver a robust and full-bodied cup and are wonderful with milk and/or sugar added to them. The New Vithanakande tea factory in southwestern Sri Lanka, which I visited in 2012, is one of the country's most famous processors of low-grown teas. It sits in the center of the Sinharaja rain forest and buys freshly harvested tea leaves from thousands of small farmers in the area. As you rise in elevation, Ceylon teas become slightly less robust but still have good body and character. The high-grown teas, while retaining some body, have a noticeably lighter character and have been known to fetch record prices.

One of the finest high-grown tea operations in the country is the Pedro Estate, located in the picturesque region of Nuwara Eliya in central Sri Lanka. It was the only estate owned by Scottish-born James Taylor, who arrived in Sri Lanka in 1852 and planted the first tea bushes in the country in the mid-1860s. Today, that historical estate yields the highly prized, delicate, fragrant Lover's Leap tea, which I find reminiscent of a first flush Darjeeling, though with its own unique characteristics defined by terroir.

But like all agricultural products, tea crops are affected by more than seasonality and elevation. Fluctuations in temperature and in rainfall amounts can create subtle and not-so-subtle changes in flavor each year—differences that dedicated tea drinkers look forward to discovering with every new harvest.

Most specialty teas are a blend of teas that have been combined to produce an optimal cup for drinking. There are three basic types of blends: Single-estate teas are blended from several days of plucking on the same estate. Lover's Leap tea from the Pedro Estate, mentioned above, is a good example. Single-origin teas are blends put together from estates within a specific area, either a region within a country or a single country. A prime example would be an Assam tea from India, which you know is from the Assam region without knowing the specific estates. Finally, some teas are the result of blending leaves from various countries. One of the most popular examples of this type of specialty tea is English breakfast tea, which is a mix of black teas from India, Sri Lanka, Kenya, and sometimes China.

HOW TEA LEAVES BECOME TEA

How the leaves from a single type of plant can be turned into six classes of tea, each with its own highly distinctive character, can seem almost like magic. We have the Chinese to thank for this sleight of hand, for they developed the now centuries-old series of steps that defines tea production today. Each step must be completed with precision, however, or the tea will not be worthy of drinking. Most important for specialty tea, the leaves must remain whole or nearly whole, a practice known as orthodox production (see "Orthodox and Nonorthodox Production," page 22).

The first step in tea production is the harvest, which is done by hand in most countries. Tea harvesters, the majority of whom are women because of their generally superior dexterity, start work very early in the morning when

Orthodox and Nonorthodox Production

When processing leaves for specialty teas, the goal is to preserve the whole leaf as much as possible. To achieve this, the manufacturer adheres to what is known as orthodox production, a method originally done by hand when the Chinese began processing tea leaves more than two millennia ago. The work continued in that fashion until the 1840s, when the British started to grow tea in India and Sri Lanka and invented machines that mimicked the hand techniques. This new equipment dramatically reduced the most labor-intensive aspects of tea processing, which quickly resulted in increased production. In time, factories in China and other tea-producing countries adopted the machines. Modernized versions of these early machines are still used today, though some highly prized specialty teas continue to be processed by hand.

In the early 1930s, the CTC (cut or crush, tear, curl) machine was invented, which sped up production even more, and it, too, remains in use. After the leaves are dried, they are fed into the CTC, where sharp blades first shred and tear them and then roll them into tiny balls. This method is known as nonorthodox production because the leaves are reduced to small spherical pieces.

A second machine, the rotovane, is sometimes used at the end of orthodox production. It cuts whole leaves into smaller pieces for both loose tea and tea bags. The pieces remain flat, rather than being compressed into balls as they are with the CTC machine. Some tea enthusiasts insist that rotovane-cut leaves are still correctly classified as products of orthodox production; others insist that once a whole leaf is deliberately cut, it no longer fits that description.

temperatures are cooler. Working quickly and carefully, the harvesters *pluck*—the term used in the tea world—the new leaves (or *flush*) and immediately drop them into bags or baskets strapped to their backs. For the finest teas, they harvest only the bud and the next two youngest leaves, a practice known as fine plucking. When one or two additional leaves are also included, the technique is called coarse plucking and yields a lower-quality tea. In a few countries, most notably Japan, the leaves are sometimes plucked by machine. Most of the finest teas are picked by hand, however, as mechanized picking can easily damage the tender shoots. The harvest is then transported to the production facility as quickly as possible before too much moisture is lost.

Two basic types of processing facility exist in the world of tea: the small cottage operation, which can be as modest as a makeshift structure in someone's backyard or a small factory, and the several-story factory at the edge of a tea-growing area that boasts tens of thousands of bushes.

Regardless of the size of the facility, the steps for making the different classes of tea are the same.

Once the harvest arrives at the processing facility, it is weighed so that its weight can be recorded and then the leaves are sorted. This initial sorting is to check that the quality of pluck has been achieved. In other words, does it meet the standard of what the tea estate manager or owner desired, such as a bud only, two leaves and a bud, or a bud and three leaves? It is also when any garden debris, like sticks or small stones that might have found their way into the tea, is discarded.

Withering is the next step in most, though not all, tea production. Its goal is to reduce the moisture content in the tea leaves and make them more pliable, and it can happen outside in the sun, outside in the shade, inside a factory, or a combination of all three. Depending on where you are in the world, the leaves might be withered in oversized bamboo baskets, in large wooden troughs with good air circulation, or on stacked rack-like shelves in a breezy factory room. During this dehydrating process, most leaves will lose roughly 20 percent of their moisture, much in the same way that a bunch of fresh-cut flowers that are not put in water right away will begin to wilt.

How long the leaves are withered depends on the class of tea being made—for example, Chinese green teas are withered only briefly, while some black teas are left for hours—and on the weather conditions, such as how hot or humid or windy it is. The timing is determined by an expert, who might be the manager of a tea estate, garden, or plantation or a formally trained tea master at the factory. If the leaves are not withered properly, they will likely break into small pieces as they undergo the subsequent processing steps, and improper withering could also damage them beyond repair for the next steps in production. Also, because the leaves change chemically as they wither, this step contributes to the final flavor of the tea. That means if the withering time is too short or too long, the tea will not taste as it should.

What happens now depends on the class of tea and on the country in which it is being made. Pan firing, also known as *chaoqing*, or "roasting out of the green," calls for tossing the leaves by hand in a hot bowl-shaped pan or turning them in a hot mechanized rotating drum that resembles a very deep clothes dryer. This step, which is used primarily for Chinese green teas, simultaneously crushes the leaves gently to release enzymes that alter their flavor and heats the leaves to prevent oxidation (browning), thus keeping the green leaves green. The makers of Japanese green teas replace both withering and pan firing with a single step, steaming, to achieve the same end.

Plucking Tea: Not as Easy as It Looks

While in Sri Lanka researching tea production, I was given an opportunity to pluck alongside some of the harvesters in the field. I had studied tea and tea processing for more than eleven years at that time, so I thought I knew the technique well. It was just a matter of putting it into practice. That assumption is what got me into trouble.

The friendly, colorfully dressed women workers first taught me how to secure the basket to my body. Each basket has a long strap that the worker affixes to the top of her head so that the basket rests on her back, leaving her hands free to pluck. The basket must remain carefully balanced and motionless as the plucker works her way through the narrow rows of bushes. As I began to walk, my basket swayed, hitting bushes on both sides, and although I really tried, I never mastered the "carefully balanced" basket for as long as it was on my back.

Next, I watched closely as the women plucked the leaves and, with precision, tossed them over their shoulders into their baskets. They worked quickly and efficiently, knowing exactly which leaves to pluck and which ones to leave alone. I started plucking and soon began to feel overwhelmed by the sea of green. It was hard to determine which shoots to pluck and which ones to leave alone. You must also make a fast twisting movement with your wrist to get a clean break from the plant. Between determining which stems to pluck from a mass of green, how to execute just the right twisting action, and trying to balance the basket with my head, I didn't get very far. The women did start to giggle a little as they patiently tried to show me each step again, and they probably went home that day and laughed about the woman from America who tried to work alongside them in the tea field.

That experience taught me two things: It convinced me that I would be a very poor tea harvester. In fact, I am sure I would be fired because I doubt that I could ever master the skills needed to meet a harvester's daily quota. I also learned that it is a lot harder to pluck tea leaves than it looks, and that I had better stick to speaking and writing about tea and entrust the harvesting of it to others.

Next, the leaves are rolled, which can be done by hand or machine. The rolling motion is as if you placed flaccid tea leaves on your flattened palm; placed your other hand, palm-side down, on top; and then gently moved your hands back and forth to roll the leaves, breaking them open so their juices seep out. The action cracks the cells of the leaf, allowing them to come in contact with oxygen that sets off oxidation. It also shapes the leaves into cylinders. The rolled leaves can then be left as cylinders, or they can then be formed into various shapes, such as cones, spirals, or balls, depending on the tea that is being made. Chinese producers regularly receive high praise for their imaginatively shaped teas.

Oxidation is what gives some teas much of their aroma, color, and flavor. The rolled and shaped leaves are spread on trays and left undisturbed so that the enzymes released during the rolling step are exposed to air. The longer the leaves are allowed to oxidize, the darker the tea will become. How much the leaves are allowed to oxidize depends on the class of tea, and how long they oxidize depends on how much heat and humidity is present. Both white teas and green teas are nonoxidized teas (though some oxidation occurs naturally), so they skip this step. Yellow and oolong teas are semioxidized, black teas are fully oxidized, and dark teas undergo a unique combined process of fermentation and oxidation.

Drying is the final step in tea processing, before the tea is packaged for sale. The leaves can be air-dried, sun-dried, turned in a pan over a hot fire, or "baked" in a hot-air machine, with the latter being the most common. Proper drying is essential to making the leaves shelf stable. That means it requires great precision: If the leaves are dried too quickly, they may remain moist at the center and begin to mold later. If the temperature is too high or too low, the optimal taste or desired color may be lost.

THE SIX CLASSES OF TEA

As noted earlier, the steps in tea production vary according to the class of tea being made, and here you will learn what those distinctions are for each of the six classes. Before you plunge into the intricacies of how each class of tea is processed, if you have not just read the previous section, "How Tea Leaves Become Tea" (page 21), read it now to refresh your memory on what happens to leaves after they are plucked and before they go into your teapot.

White Tea

Producers in China would like the international tea market to believe that white tea can come only from the downy, snow-white tender first buds of the Da Bai (large white) tea bush cultivated in Fujian Province, where the production of white tea originated. Not surprisingly, other producers, primarily in Nepal, Sri Lanka, Thailand, and India where white tea is also made and sold, disagree, insisting that white tea is defined by the process, not the bush and its location.

White tea undergoes fewer steps than any other tea class to become a salable product. The freshly plucked buds or buds and leaves are

briefly withered, during which a very light oxidation naturally occurs that turns them gray-green or gray-brown. Then, in most cases, they are moved directly to the drying step, which is done gently and under carefully controlled conditions either naturally (by air or sun) or mechanically (a hot-air machine). The simplicity of the processing belies the exceptional qualities of the tea and the high prices it commands.

There are three basic types of white tea. Silver Needle is made from lustrous, silvery buds (unopened leaf shoots) that are covered in white downy fuzz. It has a subtle, mildly sweet flavor. White Peony uses the bud along with next two youngest leaves, which contribute a sweet, mildly grassy flavor and a slight briskness. Shou Mei, made with a nonuniform mix of buds and lower-grade leaves, sometimes goes through a light rolling and an intentional light oxidation phase to deepen the flavor, resulting in a floral, fruity taste.

Green Tea

When processing green tea, it is critical that the leaves remain green, which means no oxidation must occur. This is accomplished by applying heat. Both China and Japan are famous for their green teas, but each uses a different method to prevent oxidation, and each method results in a notable difference in the color and flavor of the finished tea. Other countries that produce green teas, such as Sri Lanka, India, South Korea, and Kenya, have adopted one of these two traditional methods.

Chinese Green Tea

For Chinese green tea, the leaves are first treated to a short wither, then immediately undergo pan firing, either manually or mechanically, to halt the oxidation. At the end of this step, the leaves range from a greenish yellow to a deep green that is almost brown. In the tea world, many of the finest Chinese green teas are celebrated not only for their flavor and color but also for their beautiful shape, a quality that brings distinction to the tea maker. The shaping, which is done by hand or machine, can occur simultaneously with the pan firing or be an additional step. Some of the shapes are reflected in the names of the teas, such as Mei (eyebrow), Gua Pian (pumpkin or melon seed), Pi (Bi) Luo Chun (green spring snail), and Jian (tip or point). It is important to note that the beauty of the leaves doesn't always translate to superior taste, however.

Sometimes a second pan firing is done, depending on what final leaf style is desired. This is followed by a stint in a dryer to reduce the moisture of the finished tea. In some cases, this step imparts a slightly smoky flavor to the tea. The leaves are then sorted for size and color before sale.

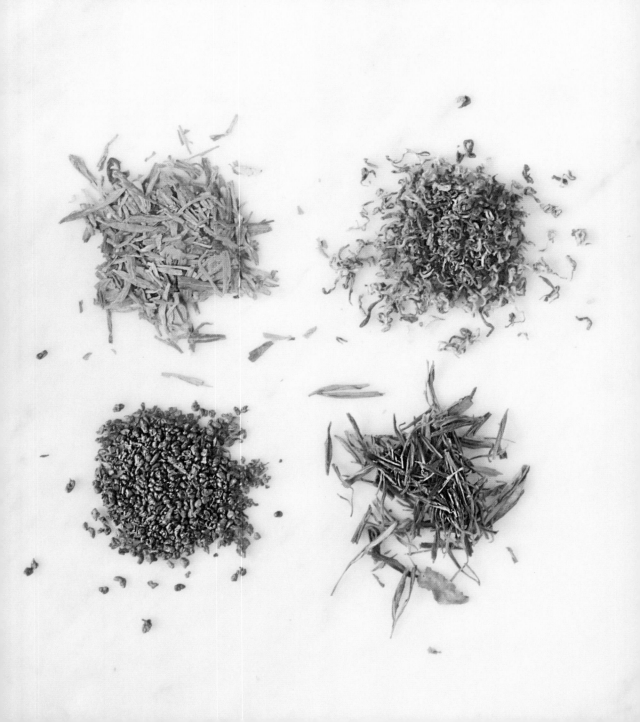

Here are some of the most famous Chinese green teas.

- **DRAGON WELL (LONGJING)**: Flat leaves with a smooth, fresh floral flavor and a slightly sweet, toasty aftertaste.

- **GUNPOWDER (ZHU CHA)**: Ball-shaped leaves that yield a smooth, medium-body tea with a touch of smoky sweetness.

- **HUANGSHAN MAOFENG**: Made from the leaf buds, with an intricate sweet and slightly grassy flavor.

- **PI (BI) LUO CHUN**: Semicurled leaves with sweet, slightly floral, and grassy flavors, sometimes with toasty notes.

Japanese Green Tea

Green tea is almost the only tea processed in Japan (a small amount of black tea is being produced), and the Japanese have long devoted great thought and care to its production. Most of the harvest is done mechanically rather than by hand, and some bushes are shaded for several weeks before harvest. This latter technique changes the flavor of the tea, a flavor that some consumers consider more desirable. Shading also alters the chemical makeup of the leaves, a topic that is explored in "What Is In Your Tea?" (page 139) and "The Buzz about Caffeine" (page 142).

Japanese green tea makers neither wither nor pan fire their leaves as the Chinese do. Instead they steam them to soften them, which also halts oxidation and begins to develop their flavor. When the leaves emerge from the steaming step, they are a bright evergreen color. I like to use the example of steaming broccoli when explaining this step. When you steam broccoli rather than stir-fry it, the color is a brighter, more intense green. This helps explain the color variation between Japanese green tea and Chinese green tea.

Next, the leaves go through an automated production of rolling, shaping, and a final drying to make them shelf stable. Unlike tea producers in most countries, the Japanese do not sort their teas by size of the leaves. The teas are blended

Japan's Tea Fields

Japan is a mix of new technology and long-standing tradition. This is evident when you visit Shizuoka Prefecture, home to Mount Fuji and where some 40 percent of the tea consumed in Japan is produced. I arrived in Tokyo by plane and then traveled with our group by train to Shizuoka, where skyscrapers lit up the night sky and the streets were crowded with fast-moving people in suits. We headed to a small, modern hotel where we all settled into rooms for the night. The next morning I peered out the window of my room and was surprised to see an ancient formal Japanese garden with statues, serene pools, manicured rock gardens, a cemetery, and a Buddhist temple, all perfectly preserved at the heart of the modern city. That diverse pairing of old and new is repeated whenever you visit tea gardens in Japan.

As our group traveled along the prefecture's modern highways, we saw tea fields—deep green patches scattered over the hills and mountains— to either side of the road. Some fields were so steep that it was difficult to imagine a person or a machine being able to harvest the leaves. Others were terraced, with sturdy rock walls holding back the soil. The cultivation of tea in Japan goes back more than a thousand years (see page 15, "Where is Tea Grown?"), but today's production methods are totally contemporary. Most of the tea is harvested by machine, which gives the bushes perfectly uniform rounded tops and the tea fields a manicured look reminiscent of a formal English garden. A large machine, somewhat like a riding lawn mower with a catcher attached to the back, shears off the tops of the bushes and collects the leaves. I also saw leaves being harvested by two people on either side of a row of tea bushes maneuvering what looked like a hedge trimmer. All of the leaves were taken to a factory where, from behind glass, I could see them being processed through the different steps, each of which was fully automated.

Our group also visited Shizuoka Cha Ichiba, the tea auction house in the region. Because we were there during the off-season, we watched a film on how tea is traditionally auctioned. It showed the broker, buyers, and sellers, each wearing different-colored hats according to their roles, and the bright chartreuse tea samples in shiny, black lacquered wooden boxes on stainless-steel tables. Then the new met the old again during the bidding process, when the centuries-old abacus appeared as the calculator of choice. As prices were negotiated, the wooden beads of the abacus were manipulated at lightning speed. When the final price was agreed on, the broker, buyer, and seller sealed the deal by clapping three times in unison, rather than shaking hands.

As we left the auction house, I once again reflected on the harmonious blend of old and new in the world of Japanese tea production, with the abacus, the colored hats, and the clapping in unison rich in tradition and the motorized tea harvester and state-of-the-art factory an embrace of the contemporary.

so that varying leaf sizes are mixed together. This results in a rich, thick, brothy tea and is one reason that Japanese green teas are different from most green teas. Japanese tea producers are also firm believers in not letting any part of the plucked leaves go to waste and use the twigs and stems in specific teas.

Here are some of the most famous sun-grown Japanese green teas.

- **SENCHA**: Bright, deep green needle-shaped tea with a sweet, slightly grassy umami profile.

- **BANCHA**: Similar to Sencha but made from a later harvest (lower-grade leaves) and with less astringency.

- **KUKICHA**: Made primarily from stems and stalks, low in astringency and caffeine, and with fresh green, bittersweet umami notes. Also known as twig tea.

- **HOJICHA**: Bancha and more rarely Sencha that has gone through an additional step of roasting over charcoal or in an electric roaster, which is tasted in the cup.

- **GENMAICHA**: Made by mixing Bancha and occasionally Sencha (with Matcha sometimes added for color) and toasted brown rice that gives the tea a distinctive savory taste.

Here are two famous shade-grown green teas.

- **GYOKURO**: Pricey and prized, with a rich, sweet taste without any bitterness and little astringency.

- **MATCHA**: Stone-ground leaves that have a sweet vegetal taste and some bitter notes. Used for the Japanese tea ceremony (see page 90).

Yellow Tea

This is the rarest class of tea by far, difficult to source because the harvest time is short, the processing is complex and time-consuming, and, until recently, China was the only producer. Yellow tea is seldom seen in the West—or even outside of China—and because of its appearance, it is often confused with green tea. Indeed, unscrupulous vendors have been known to label their green tea as yellow tea in the hope of fooling naïve shoppers in search of a high-status beverage. Yellow tea is now developing a following in the West, and because of this, other countries have begun producing it. But keep in mind that even if the processing is similar to what is done in China, yellow tea produced elsewhere will not taste the same as Chinese yellow tea because the terroir is different.

Yellow tea is traditionally made with leaf buds plucked in early spring. The buds are processed like Chinese green teas through the pan-firing step, or they are treated to a gentle heating method known as *men huan*, or "sealing yellow." Next, they are wrapped in thick paper or a dampened cloth, slipped into a wooden container or a dark place, and left to cool undisturbed. They are sometimes pan fired again, rewrapped, and again put into a container and left undisturbed. This sweltering stage is called piling. How many times the leaves are pan fired and how long they are wrapped varies with the tea maker, but the whole step usually takes three to four days. They then continue to the drying step to finish the tea.

This unique technique of pan firing leaves and then wrapping them allows the leaves to oxidize slightly, which contributes to the flavor profile of the tea and the leaf color. Some observers say that yellow tea falls somewhere between a white tea and a green tea and should not be termed a class at all. But the flavor, with sweet honeysuckle and apple notes, and the yellowish green leaves make the tea unique and deserving of class status. Three famous Chinese yellow teas are Gentleman Mountain Silver Needles, Mengding Yellow Sprout, and Huo Mountain Yellow Sprout. In 2010, the Chinese added a new, more affordable yellow tea to the market, Mount Jun Yellow Tip. The cost is lower because the harvest occurs well into spring and the tea contains two leaves and a bud instead of just buds.

Oolong Tea

The most famous oolong teas come from China and Taiwan, though other countries do make them. Oolong is probably the most difficult tea to produce because it includes all of the basic tea-processing steps and many possible variations within those steps. For example, oolong is a semioxidized tea, but the level of oxidation can range anywhere from as little as 10 percent, making it similar in appearance to a green tea, to as much as 80 percent, resulting in what looks like a black tea. Plus, achieving the oxidation often requires many laborious steps. In Taiwan, hotly contested oolong competitions are held in which tea masters submit their production to a blind tasting in the hope of not only winning the top prize but also seeing their product auctioned off for a stratospheric price.

During the withering step, the tea leaves are lightly bruised by shaking or rolling them, which allows their edges to begin oxidizing. The leaves are then rolled to continue the oxidation. The rolling stage is sometimes interrupted intermittently with pan firing to halt the oxidization temporarily. This alternation between rolling and heating is often repeated many times to develop the layers of flavor for which oolongs are famous.

Depending on the type of oolong being made, sometimes no further oxidation is needed, such as in the case of a Baozhong (Pouchong). For oolongs that require greater oxidation such as Da Hong Pao (Big Red Robe) and Bai Hao (Oriental Beauty, White Silver Tip, or Silver Tip), the rolled leaves are left to rest, usually on large bamboo trays, for a period of a few hours. A final drying is done by pan firing, which stops the oxidation and reduces the moisture content. These oolongs all have a long lovely twisted shape to them.

All of these painstaking steps are carefully monitored by the tea master, who decides when the leaves are moved to the next level of production. To make those decisions, the master must rely primarily on the aroma of the leaves, a skill learned over time. When I was in Taiwan making oolong, I was fascinated that the tea master knew just by the aroma of the leaf when to move to the next step.

Some oolongs, such as the famed Tung Ting (Dong Ding) and Tie Guanyin (Ti Guan Yin or Tie Kuan Yin), go through an extra step: The leaves are collected in a canvas bag, the bag is tightly gathered into a sphere the size of a bowling ball, and then the bag is repeatedly rolled by hand, by foot, or by machine. The leaves are removed from the bag, briefly heated in a tumbling machine, and then returned to the bag and rolled again. This might be done up to thirty times. The process shapes the leaves into small balls and adds a wonderful depth of flavor to the tea. A final drying is done by pan firing, which stops the oxidation and reduces the moisture content for packaging.

In some cases, the semiballed, lightly oxidized finished tea that is defined as jade oolong is lightly baked in a low oven for more depth of flavor and a toasty accent. This changes the classification from a jade oolong to an amber oolong. (Not to be confusing, but in the tea industry, amber oolongs can also be defined as any oolong that has an oxidation level higher than 25 percent. So amber oolongs are either ones that have been treated to an additional baking process or ones that have a darker color due to a longer oxidation time.) Some oolongs are treated to this same baking step annually to draw out the moisture and give the tea a smooth, unique richness. Known as aged oolongs, these teas are among the exceptions to the rule that tea is best consumed within a year or so of processing. Don't try to create an aged oolong yourself, however. This baking step requires a specially designed oven and a trained professional.

Here are some of the best-known oolong teas.

- **BAOZHONG**: Sometimes labeled Pouchong, a lightly oxidized tea, this one is twisted rather than ball-shaped, with a delicate, fresh flavor and notes of lilac.

- **TUNG TING**: A jade ball-style green-leaved tea with a sweet, silky, floral flavor. Sometimes labeled Dong Ding. If the additional final baking step has been done, it would be called an amber Tung Ting, which would yield a highly complex cup with honey notes layered with rich, dark, slightly toasty flavors.

- **TIE GUANYIN**: Known in English as Iron Goddess of Mercy (and often spelled Tie Guan Yin, Tie Kuan Yin, or Ti Kwan Yin), this popular ball-style oolong is sometimes finished with baking (the classic style), which imparts a mix of sweet dried apricot and toasty notes. A more modern-style version is less oxidized and has a sweeter flavor.

- **DA HONG PAO**: Known in English as Big Red Robe, the long, dark twisted leaves carry complex notes of fruit and sweet, as well as minerals from the rocky terrain where the plants are grown.

- **BAI HAO**: Also known as White Tip, Silver Tip, or Oriental Beauty, these big, long, dark leaves impart a sweet, fruity, floral character in the cup.

Making Tung Ting Oolong

The first time I smelled freshly plucked tea leaves was in the beautiful mountains of central Taiwan near Sun Moon Lake, where I was researching tea with a group of professionals led by Thomas Shu of ABC Tea. It was there that I was able to make tea side by side with renowned tea master Steve Huang, who was in such demand that he was booked five years in advance. The workers had brought in the freshly plucked tea leaves from the fields just before we all arrived, and the leaves were lying out in the sun to wither. Their smell was intoxicating and reminded me of honeysuckle or orange blossoms. It amazed me how floral a simple tea leaf could smell.

The leaves were put on large, flat bamboo baskets, brought indoors, and placed on racks. Working with the tea master, we gently bruised the leaves by fluffing them several times. The precision demanded by this task was unexpected. And each time I handled the leaves, I was once again intoxicated by their fragrance. The leaves were then left to rest as they oxidized.

Twelve hours had passed since we had started work, and although I was getting tired, I watched with exhilaration as the leaves underwent the pan firing, rolling, and drying processes. After a much-needed brief sleep, I returned to the factory to see what I now called "my leaves." The tea master was already at work overseeing the additional step of alternately rolling the leaves in canvas bags and pan firing them. By the time the tea was finished, almost twenty-two hours had passed from my first sight of the freshly plucked leaves.

My appreciation for tea makers grew exponentially that day. I was told that by the time a consumer drinks a cup of specialty tea, eight hundred people have put effort into getting it there. Now, every time I sip an oolong, I am taken back to Taiwan and that extraordinary tea-making experience.

Black Tea

Probably the most common class of tea consumed in the West is black tea. A fully oxidized tea, it was most likely developed by the Chinese during the Ming Dynasty (1368–1644) for export to Western markets because it was known to stand up to a long journey. Even today, black tea, which is referred to as red tea in China, isn't commonly imbibed there. Black teas are grown and processed all over the world, however, and each country's tea has a unique flavor profile.

Although many of the basic steps are the same, the processing of black tea is more straightforward than the processing of oolong tea. After the tea leaves are allowed to wither, they are rolled, but only once. The oxidation process follows, during which the rolled tea leaves are spread out on trays, racks, or raised concrete slabs and allowed to rest. As they oxidize, the leaves turn a dark brown. The final drying halts the oxidation. The leaves are then sorted into grades.

The name grading of black teas was introduced by the British to describe the physical characteristics of the leaves, and today this grading system is used primarily only in Sri Lanka and India. They are subject to each estate's interpretation and thus can be somewhat confusing. Letters are used to depict a characteristic that starts with the size of the leaf. A full-leaf tea is known as Orange Pekoe or OP. (Contrary to popular belief, this term does not indicate flavor, only size.) A broken leaf is labeled BOP. Other terms, such as Tippy (T) and Golden (G), refer to color and leaf tips. Don't concern yourself with these classifications too much, as they are subjective to each estate, and the true flavor of a tea can be evaluated only by the infusion.

These are some of the most common specialty black teas on the market.

- **ASSAM**: Grown at low elevation in northeastern India and famous for its malty flavor.

- **CEYLON**: Grown in low, middle, and high elevations in Sri Lanka. Low-grown Ceylons are bold and have good strength; mid-grown teas are rich, with a little less boldness in the cup; and high-grown teas are the most delicate and smooth and carry floral notes. (For more on Ceylon teas, see page 19, "What Is Specialty Tea?")

- **DARJEELING**: Grown in the Indian region of the same name, the flavor profile of a Darjeeling varies with the time of harvest, with the first flush revealing peachy, honey, muscatel notes and high astringency; the second flush displaying medium body, less astringency, and citrusy, crisp, apricot notes; and the autumnal flush delivering

Making Black Tea in Sri Lanka

I didn't have to use much imagination to picture what Sri Lanka was like soon after the British started growing tea there in the 1860s, when the country was known as Ceylon (its name was changed in 1972, though the tea is still called Ceylon). Evidence of a century and a half of British colonialism is readily visible in the architecture and customs of this tropical Asian island, just off the southeastern coast of India.

It was 2012 and I was traveling with a small group of tea professionals. As we made our way up a mountain and through the Valley of Bogawantalawa, known as the Golden Valley of Ceylon Tea, tea estates could be seen in every direction. We were headed to the Kotiyagala Estate, which sits at 5,000 ft/1,500 m and is arguably one of the finest estates in the valley, where we scheduled to stay for a few nights. Kotiyagala, which means "leopard rock," is so named because for years leopards have been seen coming out of the adjacent forest and resting on the rock plateau that borders the edge of the estate.

As we drove up to the estate manager's bungalow, it was like stepping back in time. Surrounded by beautiful flowers, the traditional English cottage sat at the center of the tea fields. Inside the bungalow, little appeared to have been changed since its construction in 1875. We were served tea in the sunroom, with its cane chairs, golden teak

floor, and a view of the blooming flower garden and the tea fields beyond.

Over tea, the estate manager, Mr. Dushan Jayan, explained the system from planting and pruning to processing. Then we headed to the nursery where we learned about vegetative propagation, in which cuttings are taken from mother bushes to make new plants. From the nursery, we drove to a field that was being heavily pruned. I even got to try my hand at pruning a tea bush, which is skilled hard work typically done by men. After dinner, we were taken to the factory to see the day's last batch of tea leaves in the early stages of the withering process. Tea factories in Sri Lanka are typically several stories high, with the withering troughs on the top floor in a large room outfitted with big fans to keep the air circulating so the tea does not rot. With the withering well under way, we returned to our quarters for a nightcap of locally distilled arrack (made from the sap of coconut palm flowers) and then headed off to bed, but not before a discussion on what time bed tea was to be served.

Bed tea is a marvelous tradition that guests who stay on the estate enjoy. A member of the house staff brings a rolling tea cart to your room at your desired wake-up time. The cart carries a china teapot full of freshly brewed tea, china cups and saucers, milk, sugar, spoons, and napkins. This isn't just any pot of tea, however. It is the most recently processed tea from the estate. It doesn't get any fresher than that! It is a true delight to wake up to freshly brewed tea made from the estate's latest harvest and to sip it while looking out at the tea fields that yielded it.

Early the next morning, we headed back to the factory to see how much the tea leaves had withered. As we walked into the factory, the aroma of withering leaves filled the air with a fresh floral scent. Our leaves had been withering for about twelve hours and were not quite ready for the next step, so we returned to the bungalow for a hearty breakfast of spicy curries, two kinds of rice, egg hoppers (egg-topped thin rice-flour pancakes), fried roti, bananas, and more hot tea. We were now ready to continue making tea.

After the withering step, the leaves were dropped down a shoot to the next floor and into large rolling machines (much larger than those I had seen in Taiwan) that mimic the gentle motion of rubbing the leaves between your palms. As their juices were released, the leaves began to turn from emerald green to warm brown. Next, the leaves were spread out on raised, cool concrete beds to oxidize fully. Finally, they were put on a conveyor belt and run through a large dryer to evaporate almost all of their moisture.

An integral part of the tea-making process is cupping (see page 79, "Professional Cupping"), and I was fortunate to able to stand alongside Mr. Jayan as we all cupped the tea we had just watched being made. I watched closely and listened carefully as he cupped the tea and described what he was looking for and tasting in each sample and whether or not it met the expectations of the buyer for whom the tea was being made. This would be only the first of many cuppings of this tea along the supply train.

In addition to observing the entire tea-making process, from the propagation to the cupping, we were shown all of the facilities on the estate. This type of operation is said to cover the worker "from womb to tomb," and indeed, it is a whole community, with a hospital, day care, school, and housing for the workers, supervisory staff, and their families, which numbered more than thirteen hundred people. The estate itself is beautiful, but life on it is full of hard work and is far different from anything I had known before.

full body and hints of ripe fruit and briskness. These teas are sometimes referred to as the Champagne of the tea world. (For more on Darjeeling teas, see page 19, "What Is Specialty Tea?")

- **KEEMUN**: Smooth, semisweet Chinese tea with hints of subtle smoky flavor; sometimes described as the Burgundy wine of the tea world.

- **YUNNAN**: Rich-bodied, slightly spicy Chinese tea with notes of chocolate and sweet raisin.

Dark Tea

Dark tea has its origins in China, and what sets it apart from teas in other classes is an added fermentation step. In the past, this class of tea was called Pu'erh, but in recent years, the Western specialty tea world has discovered tea in China's Hunan Province that is made essentially the same way as Pu'erh, prompting the new class name. Both Pu'erh, which originated in Yunnan Province, and the similar Hunan tea are known in China as *hei cha*, meaning "dark tea" or "black tea." (Remember, what the Western world calls black tea the Chinese refer to as red tea.) *Hei cha* of varying quality is also produced in Sichuan, Guangxi, and other provinces.

Dark tea goes through a primary production similar to that of Chinese green tea. Then the leaves are allowed to undergo microbial fermentation and further oxidation. This secondary production reportedly occurred accidentally thousands of years ago when tea was being transported on the backs of men and horses traveling from Yunnan to Tibet and Sichuan on what was known as Tea Horse Road. To prevent the leaves from crumbling during the long journey, they were moistened with water. Because the leaves were also exposed to diverse weather conditions, they were fermenting and oxidizing throughout the trip, changing from their original flavor and chemical composition to something quite different.

Today, tea makers use controlled fermentation to achieve the desired flavor, aroma, and appearance of dark tea. The details as to how this fermentation is accomplished vary from one area to another, and many specifics are deliberately kept secret. Sometimes the term *fermentation* is mistakenly used to describe the process that is actually oxidation. This mix-up comes from translating the Chinese term *fa xiao* (or *fa jiao*) as both "to oxidize" and "to ferment," even though the English words mean very different things. Oxidation has been defined earlier in this chapter (see page 21, "How Tea Leaves Become Tea"). Fermentation is the chemical breakdown of a substance by bacteria, yeasts, or other microorganisms, typically involving effervescence and the giving off of heat. As already noted, all dark teas undergo both oxidation and fermentation.

There are two types of Pu'erh: Sheng Pu'erh (raw, uncooked, or green type) and Shou Pu'erh (ripened, cooked, or black type). For both types, the tea leaves are spread in the sun or in a dry, breezy area to wither and reduce their moisture and then pan fired to stop the oxidation. Next, they are rolled and shaped into narrow strips, bruising them gently in the process, and then left in the sun to dry, where they lightly oxidize due to the bruising. They go through a second rolling and then are sorted. At this stage, the tea is called *mao cha*, or "rough tea."

For Sheng Pu'erh, the tea is stored in a controlled setting that permits the tea to age naturally, allowing fermentation to occur. This aging over time lets the flavor and aroma develop. The longer it is allowed to mature, the more complex the flavor becomes. It changes from being rather green and astringent to a darker color with a smooth, slightly earthy flavor. How long the leaves are aged varies, with two to three years a common starting point and some aging for more than twenty-five years. Not surprisingly, the superior-flavored longer-aged Sheng Pu'erh teas command higher prices.

To speed up the aging process to meet demand, Shou Pu'erh was developed in the early 1970s to approximate a long-aged Sheng Pu'erh. The rough tea is made the same way until it reaches the drying step. Instead of being left to age, the leaves are moistened with water and arranged in a large pile in a warm, humid area. The pile is closely monitored and turned as needed to encourage the microbial and fungal fermentation, much the same way a backyard compost pile is turned as it ripens. Unlike a compost pile, however, the tea leaves must not be allowed to decompose. The exact time and details for this sped-up aging process are a tightly held secret. In fact, I have had tea colleagues visit the region in Yunnan where Shou and Sheng Pu'erh is made and not be allowed into the factories.

Dark teas are sold in either loose form or compressed into various shapes during processing, such as a disk (*bingcha*), bowl (*tuocha*), or brick (*zhuancha*). If the tea is compressed into a hard shape you may need a special knife to break off pieces for steeping. Pu'erhs are smooth, rich, and earthy, with little to no astringency. If stored properly, the Sheng type will age further, developing a smoother, rounder, sweeter finish. Shou Pu'erh can also be stored, though its flavor will improve very little because the tea has not been naturally aged. Hunan dark teas are less earthy than Pu'erh teas and have a smooth, slightly sweet floral flavor. They are regarded as everyday teas and are meant to be imbibed when purchased. The aroma of all dark tea leaves can be somewhat off-putting. These teas taste much differently than they smell, however, so they are worth exploring and are an especially good choice after a heavy meal.

CHAPTER TWO

THE ART OF TEA

Buying, Storing, Steeping, and Tasting

Specialty tea, which you read about in depth in chapter one, is an affordable luxury that you can treat yourself to every day. But to do that well, you must first learn some basics, including how to shop for tea and tea paraphernalia, how to store tea once you get it home, how to steep it so that it shows off its character, and how to appreciate its flavor nuances so that every cup is memorable.

THE ART OF BUYING TEA

Now that you understand what distinguishes each of the six classes of tea (see "The Six Classes of Tea," pages 26 to 46), the next step is to find some good-quality teas that you enjoy drinking. There are many similarities between shopping for fine wines and fine teas, so if you are a serious wine buyer, you will be able to apply much of what you know to your tea shopping.

Just as going to a wine tasting is a good way to discover new wines, attending a tea tasting is likely to introduce you to teas that you have never tried before. If there is a respected teahouse or specialty tea retailer in your area, ask if tastings are held there. If there isn't one in your area, search online to see if you can find something within a reasonable distance. Checking out tastings may be something you want to do when you travel or take vacations, too. I usually research retailers and teahouses before I leave on a trip. It is an interesting way not only to learn about new teas but also to experience part of the culture of a city or town that most travelers will never know.

The staff at any good specialty tea retailer will be able to talk knowledgeably about what the store carries and guide you to some teas you may like.

But just as with buying wine, trial and error is the only way to discover which teas you enjoy the most. The dozens of choices in a shop can seem overwhelming, however, so my advice is to start with what you are familiar with and branch out from there. If you know you like black teas from China's Fujian Province, for example, the clerk can direct you toward black teas from a different province, such as Yunnan, or from a different country, such as India. Or you might try experimenting according to a specific flavor profile. If you prefer a hearty black tea to which you can add milk and sugar, for instance, the clerk can introduce you to a handful of choices that fit that description, such as Ceylon from Sri Lanka, an Assam from India, or a blended tea, like English Breakfast. Fruity teas, of which there are many, are yet another group to explore. Tea drinkers who like these teas, which includes such popular choices as a Black Lychee, Tropical Green, or black tea flavored with citrus, usually stock up on a selection of them so that they have a variety from which to choose when they crave a cup at home.

Many people begin their tea drinking with flavored teas or tisanes and then develop a taste for unflavored high-end straight teas later. Again, this is similar to serious wine drinkers, who are seldom still drinking their first wine. As I mentioned earlier, when I was first became interested in tea, my favorite was a black cinnamon-spiced raspberry-flavored tea. I still like it, though

Scented and Flavored Teas

Any class of tea can be scented or flavored, thanks to its hygroscopic properties, that is, the ability to absorb fragrances as well as moisture from the air. This is bad if tea is stored improperly, of course. But it's good if you want to infuse teas with wonderful aromas and flavors. There is a big difference between scented and flavored teas, however.

Scented teas are made by exposing a finished tea to a desirable scent, such as that of rose, osmanthus, or jasmine flowers. Jasmine Pearl tea, for example, is made by rolling green tea into small "pearls," drying it, mixing it with freshly picked jasmine flowers to infuse it, and then separating the tea and blossoms and drying the tea again to eliminate any moisture absorbed from the jasmine. This process is repeated a few times, with new blossoms each time, until the tea is fragrant with jasmine. Tea can also be scented with smoke, such as the highly regarded Lapsang Souchong from China's Fujian Province, which gets its distinctive smoky character from exposing black tea to the smoke from a pine wood fire. Not surprisingly, some tea makers use shortcuts to make scented teas, relying on liquid flavor agents.

Flavored teas are made by adding a flavoring oil or other flavoring agent. The famed Earl Grey tea, which is black tea infused with either bergamot peel or, more commonly, bergamot oil, is among the best-known examples. Mango, citrus, peach, and raspberry are other typical flavorings. Spice- or herb-flavored teas are also popular, such as Masala Chai, which typically blends cardamom, cinnamon, cloves, ginger, and other spices with black tea.

mostly for iced tea on a hot day. I have moved on to discover many teas that don't have any added flavorings but can taste mysteriously like chocolate, honeysuckle, or melon on their own. It is a quest of mine now to find teas that I have never tasted and to detect the special nuances in each one. Drinking tea should be enjoyable to you, so if you want to stick with what you already love, that's okay. But I encourage you to try teas that are outside your realm of familiarity. Doing so is like anything new: You don't know if you like it until you try it. There are hundreds of teas to choose from, and exploring them is exciting.

Once you find some teas you like at a tea shop, buy in small quantities, and, if possible, always try one new kind of tea to expand your repertoire. Keeping the amounts small is a good idea for a couple of reasons. It allows you to go home with a few different types of tea at one time and ensures that you will finish them before they begin to lose their flavor. Also, if you find that you don't care for the new tea, you will not have invested much in it. If instead you love it, you can always go back for more. A cup of fine tea is truly an affordable luxury, and picking up a few wonderful teas is not overly costly. For example,

buying tea in larger quantities such as one pound or a half kilo may seem to demand an exorbitantly expensive price at first look. But, the cost per serving size ends up being only small pocket change in reality, since it will make roughly two hundred cups of tea.

If you have visited a specialty tea shop outside your area and like the stock and the staff, check to see if the shop will ship teas to you. If the shop will send them but does not have a website for online ordering, ask for a list of their offerings. That way, you can order over the phone the next time. Once you have developed a good relationship with a tea purveyor, you may feel comfortable occasionally asking for a small sample of a new tea to try.

If you live in a place that doesn't have a specialty tea store and traveling isn't an option, try visiting a modest-size specialty food store that carries teas. Oftentimes one or more staff members will know about the teas that the store stocks. Unfortunately, I have found that most large specialty food stores often lack a knowledgeable tea staff. That means that you are on your own, and a long aisle stocked with countless teas can be daunting. In this case, my advice is to look for your favorite type of tea and buy that type in a few different brands. At home, do a side-by-side comparison of the teas to find which brand you prefer. Then, the next time you go to the store, pick up a few more different types of teas from

the same company. Be daring and try something you may never have heard of before. You will soon discover what you like.

The final option is to purchase your teas online. Start with the companies that I have listed in the Resources (page 156). All of them are reputable operations, and I know the principals at many of them personally. Again, I suggest that you order in small quantities and perhaps begin with just two or three teas. If you like what you order, you can order more. Also, you may be able to talk with a sales representative over the phone to help you with your next purchase. Explain what you've liked, and perhaps he or she can direct you to other teas that you may want to try. With a bit of luck, you will begin to develop a good long-distance relationship with your online tea shop just as you would with a nearby brick-and-mortar store.

Whether you are shopping in a store or online, keep in mind that some teas are seasonal, and your tea purveyor may run out of the current year's supply. Always ask if the teas you have chosen fall under this description. That way, you can plan ahead to buy more before a favorite disappears.

Now that you have read through these simple, practical shopping tips, you are ready to begin stocking your tea pantry. Aim for a variety of teas to meet every need, depending on your mood, the meal you are eating, the season of the year, the time of day, and more.

Most tea shops and online tea purveyors also sell tea accessories, and shopping for them can be fun. I am always on the lookout for something unusual that will make my tea experience more enjoyable. In "The Art of Steeping Tea," page 57, I describe what you need to make tea, and you'll find that you don't need much to make a perfect cup. But you may find enjoyment in collecting teaware and various accessories, as there are many different styles of pots, cups, and infusers on the market. Also, depending on how much you begin to experiment with different teas or tea ceremonies (see chapter three), you may want to have a variety of different tea services on hand for each occasion, ceremony, or class of tea.

THE ART OF STORING TEA

Once you have purchased fine teas and brought them home, you want to be sure you store them properly. Most teas should be consumed within a year or so of purchase, depending on how fresh the tea was when you bought it. This is not because tea goes bad, but rather because it will lose its flavor over time. An exception to this

would be Matcha, which should be used within three months or so upon opening.

Store all of your teas away from light in a cool, dry place with a moderate, consistent temperature. As I mentioned in "Scented and Flavored Teas" on page 52, tea is hygroscopic; that is, it absorbs moisture from the air and odors and fragrances in the surrounding area. This quality is a good thing when a tea maker is trying to scent or flavor the tea. But it is a bad thing when your newly purchased favorite tea tastes just like coffee because you thought it would be convenient to put them in the same cabinet.

Enclose the tea in an airtight container. It can be a ceramic canister, a tin, or a foil pouch. Sometimes I buy teas in large quantities, so I like to divide up each tea into smaller units. This is because each time you open a container, the tea is exposed to moisture and loses some of its freshness.

Even though you have put your tea in a well-sealed container, it is best not to store it near anything that is highly fragrant, such as coffee or cinnamon or other spices. Nor should you store it near a highly fragrant tea, such as Masala Chai. I have a cabinet devoted to tea storage, and in it, I am careful to have my scented and flavored teas, sealed airtight, on a separate shelf.

As with rules about most things, there are exceptions. For example, when it comes to Japanese Matcha, which is finely ground green tea leaves, there are varying schools of thought on proper storage. It should be stored in a tightly closed container in a cool dry place, but some vendors suggest storing it in the refrigerator or even the freezer as long as as it is not contaminated by moisture from either. Dark teas are another exception. Because they go through a secondary processing during which they ferment, dark teas are actually living things. Store them in a cool place with a little touch of humidity and good air circulation so they can breathe. Keep in mind that you want this area to be free of other odors that may find their way into your dark teas. Also, a few teas get better over time if stored properly, such as Sheng Pu'erhs and aged amber oolongs.

THE ART OF STEEPING TEA

Steeping tea is not complicated, nor does it require a lot of specialized equipment. In fact, you will need only a few things to get started. This is not to say that once you get hooked on tea, you won't want to buy more equipment or want to upgrade what you already own! But that's what happens with most things you enjoy.

For now, you need only the bare necessities: tea, which you have already purchased; water; a kettle; and a teapot.

Water

If you don't like the look or taste of your tap water, you will not want to use it for making tea. If you are not convinced it will make a difference, do a side-by-side comparison by making tea with your tap water and then with filtered water. Depending on where you live, the difference in flavor can be huge.

Three basic things affect the flavor of tap water: its mineral content, how hard it is, and its alkalinity, or pH. For water geeks, there is an ideal water recipe—who knew?—for making tea: 150 ppm (parts per million) total dissolved solids (mineral content), 85 ppm (5 grains) hardness, and 40 ppm (7 pH, or neutral) alkalinity, no color, no iron, no silica, and a clean taste.

Of course, most tap water does not fit this standard of perfection and cannot be filtered to achieve it. But you can filter your water to reduce its chlorine content and remove common impurities, which will improve its taste. You don't need to invest in an expensive filtration system; most inexpensive ones will do a good job. Purchasing spring water is an option, too, though many spring waters are high in mineral content and pH. Never use distilled water, as it lacks the oxygen that tea requires during steeping. If you do use it, your tea will taste flat.

Kettle

A simple stove-top kettle is fine to get you started. You will need an instant-read thermometer to make sure the water is the correct temperature for the tea you are making, or you will need to watch the water for signs that it is at the optimal temperature. How to judge if the water has reached a specific temperature is described on page 65 ("How to Determine Water Temperature by Sight"). If you especially enjoy brewing different classes of tea, you may want to invest in an electric adjustable-thermostat kettle (see Resources, page 156). They aren't too pricey and are highly convenient. I have one and I love it.

Teapot

A teapot does not have to be a big investment, either. I prefer to steep my tea in a pot made of glass, ceramic, porcelain, or bone china. The size and shape are up to you, though some conventions apply if you are making tea in either the traditional Eastern or Western style, both of which are described on pages 61 and 62. If you are happy making tea without regard to custom, you can make it in almost any vessel that can withstand boiling or hot water or both.

Infuser

If you are buying loose-leaf tea and want to make it in the Western style, you will need some type of infuser so that you can remove the leaves after the tea has steeped. I prefer an infuser that allows enough room for the leaves to expand fully, which is sometimes three to five times the original volume of the dried leaves. This spreading out is called "the agonizing of the leaves," and it is when tea gives up all of its wonderful flavor. If your infuser is too small, the leaves cannot open fully, and your tea won't realize its taste potential.

My favorite materials for infusers are glass or stainless steel. You can also purchase fill-your-own paper tea sacks made of unbleached paper that are especially good for travel. I don't recommend a tea ball, because they are simply too small.

HOW TO MAKE HOT TEA

You are now ready to begin making tea. I wish there was one set way to steep all tea, but there isn't. Because the six classes of teas are the products of six different production methods, they must be treated individually when it is time to steep them. Here is where science mixes with art. These are only guidelines, of course. This is your tea to enjoy, so make it first according to the rules and then vary them depending on your palate.

You may have seen teapots and teacups for Eastern- and Western-style tea making displayed side by side in a shop and wondered why the Eastern pots and cups were so small when compared with their Western counterparts. That's because the tea is steeped differently in the two styles.

Eastern Style

In the Eastern style, straight tea is generally used, that is, tea without added flavorings or scents. You use much more tea than for the Western style, and it is steeped for a shorter period of time. This allows for many more infusions with the same leaves, with each infusion bringing out a unique flavor. The same tea leaves are repeatedly infused until their flavor has been exhausted, then the teapot is emptied of the spent leaves, which eliminates the need for an infuser. Details on how to steep tea in the Eastern style appear in chapter three, where the Chinese tea ceremony is fully explained.

Some small Asian-style teapots are not glazed. If you have one or more these pots, use each pot for only one class of tea. This is because unglazed pots will absorb the flavor of the tea, which will muddle the taste of any other class of tea you steep in the same pot. The water-temperature guidelines remain the same whether you are using a glazed or unglazed pot.

Western Style

In the Western style, the pots are larger, less tea is used for each pot, the tea is put into an infuser, and the steeping time is longer than in the Eastern style. Plus, both unflavored and flavored teas are used and more than one infusion is relatively uncommon. Oolong, green, and dark teas may yield more than one pot of tea with the same leaves, but more than two pots is unlikely. Since you are using a smaller amount of leaves and the steeping time is longer, you will have to experiment by steeping multiple pots to know how many infusions are possible.

Many tea connoisseurs will tell you the best way to know how much tea to use when making tea Western style is to weigh 2 or 3 grams of dry leaves for each 6 oz/170 ml water. If this level of precision is becoming your tea path, I encourage you to buy a small metric digital scale and forge ahead. Most tea drinkers, however, will leave buying a scale and weighing tea to the connoisseurs.

So, if you don't want to weigh the tea, what is the best way to judge how much to use? The old adage of using a rounded 1 teaspoon per cup is a good place to start. This is an actual measuring spoon, not the type in your silverware drawer. There is some degree of variance on the measuring, however. If the tea leaves are small or broken, they will take up less room by volume than if the tea leaves are large and whole. For example, White Peony tea has more volume by weight, so I would use a heaping 2 teaspoons per cup. Let your eye and your palate guide you in how much tea you like per cup.

Bill Waddington, the owner of TeaSource, a wholesale and retail specialty tea company, is a well-respected tea expert in the United States. He is also a friend of mine and has a wonderful way of expressing how people should understand tea making. He says, "One of the most important pieces of advice I give folks who are new to tea is to realize that tea is food, plain and simple. And different people like the same food prepared in different ways. Some folks like their steak well-done and some like it rare. How do you know how you like your steak? My guess is that you have tried steak cooked several ways and have decided what the best way is for you. The same is true of tea. You should experiment with your tea and have the pleasure of figuring out how you like it!" A second good piece of advice is to keep in mind how water temperature affects the outcome: the hotter the water, the more body and strength you will get in your cup, and the cooler the water, the more sweetness and aroma.

Never Boil the Same Water Twice

If you are boiling water for a second pot or to infuse leaves a second time, be sure to start with fresh water. Water has minerals and gases that come from the earth and the atmosphere. The carbon dioxide it contains gives it a slight acidity, which influences its color and taste. When water boils for a while, it slowly loses it carbon dioxide, which makes it less acidic. That loss gives steeped tea a different color and strength that are not optimal.

Only with experimentation can you find what you really like. You might decide you like a certain class of tea to bring out body and another class of tea to bring out sweetness. Have fun discovering how you like your perfect cup of tea. This chart is a guide to get you started. Note that there is a range for the water temperature and for the steeping time. This is because a great cup of tea is for *you* to decide!

Water Temperatures and Steeping Times

Tea Class	Water Temperature	Steeping Time
White	180°–190°F/ 82°–88°C	3–5 minutes
Japanese green	160°–170°F/ 71°–77°C	30 seconds– 1½ minutes
Chinese green	170°–180°F/ 77°–82°C	2–3 minutes
Yellow	170°–180°F/ 77°–82°C	1–2 minutes
Oolong (varies greatly in oxidation and shape, so need to experiment)	180°–200°F/ 82°–93°C	3–5 minutes
Most black except Darjeeling	205°–212°F/ 96°–100°C	3–5 minutes
Darjeeling	200°–205°F/ 93°–96°C	2½– 4 minutes
Dark	205°–212°F/ 96°–100°C	3–6 minutes
Herbals or Tisanes	212°F/100°C	5–10 minutes

How to Determine Water Temperature by Sight

If you don't have an instant-read thermometer or an electric kettle with an adjustable thermostat, you can determine the temperature of water by sight. The Chinese use descriptive terminology, much of which draws on sea life, as described in the chart below. If you are reluctant to trust judging by eye, you can instead bring the water to a boil, turn off the heat, remove the lid from the kettle, and let the water rest for a specific amount of time. Those times are included in the chart as well.

Water Temperature	The Look of the Water	Resting Time after Reaching a Boil
160°–170°F/ 71°–77°C	**SHRIMP EYES:** Tiny bubbles the size of a pinhead that resemble shrimp eyes begin to rise to the surface and pop. A slow and gentle vapor of steam is visible.	5 minutes
170°–180°F/ 77°–82°C	**CRAB EYES:** Water bubbles about the size of crab eyes and vertical streams of steam rise upward.	3 minutes
180°–190°F/ 82°–88°C	**FISH EYES:** Bubbles the size of a pearl reach the top and much more steam is present than with crab eyes.	2 minutes
195°–205°F/ 90°–96°C	**ROPE OF PEARLS:** Bubbles are connected to one another in a steady stream.	1 minute
212°F/100°C	**RAGING TORRENT:** Water is at a full boil with a constant stream of large, swirling bubbles.	n/a

HOW TO MAKE ICED TEA

In the United States, iced tea is popular just about everywhere and accounts for more than 80 percent of the tea consumed in the country. Although iced tea is enjoyed in other parts of the world, such as Germany, Austria, Malaysia, and Japan, it is not imbibed at nearly the same level as in the United States. If you are not familiar with making and drinking iced tea, you might want to experiment. It can be incredibly refreshing whenever the temperature rises, and it can be made with any kind of tea. I especially like using black, green, and oolong. It is simple to make, easy to store, and wonderful to pack for picnics and road trips.

Here are two basic ways to make iced tea: hot brewed, which yields nearly instant results, and cold brewed, which takes at least eight hours. The difference in timing is because it takes much longer to extract the flavor compounds in cold water. You also use a smaller amount of leaves when cold brewing, and the tea has a noticeably lighter, smoother flavor. Either of these basic ways of making iced tea can be adapted to the size of the pitcher or jug you are using. Making iced tea isn't an exact recipe and depends greatly on the strength of the brew you like.

Sun tea, which calls for pouring cold water over tea leaves or tea bags and leaving the container in direct sun for several hours, is a third popular method for brewing iced tea. I do not recommend this method, however. It can be dangerous to leave water sitting in the sun for an extended period because of the growth of potentially harmful bacteria as the water temperature rises.

HOT BREW METHOD FOR ICED TEA: To make 1 gl/4 L iced tea, measure about 1/3 cup/25 g tea leaves. Remember to adjust for the size of the leaves, adding more if they are large and fewer if they are small. You might also need to adjust depending on the strength you desire. Put the leaves into a large infuser and put the infuser into a teapot or a 1-gl/4-L heatproof pitcher. Following the guidelines in the steeping chart on page 64, add hot water and steep according to the class of tea you are using. Remove the infuser when the specified time has passed. If using a teapot, decant the tea into a heat-proof pitcher. If you like to sweeten your tea, add sugar in the amount desired and stir to dissolve. Fill the pitcher with water or ice or both. If the tea is not cold enough when serving, add ice to the glasses.

COLD BREW METHOD FOR ICED TEA: To make 1 gl/4 L iced tea, measure a rounded 3 table-spoons tea leaves. Remember to adjust for the size of the leaves, adding more if they are large and fewer if they are small. Put the leaves into a large infuser or directly into a 1-gl/4-L pitcher or jug. Fill the container with cold water, cover, and refrigerate to infuse for at least 8 hours or up to overnight. Just before serving, remove the infuser or strain the tea into another container. Serve the tea over ice. If you like sweetened iced tea, you'll need to make a simple syrup, as sugar does not dissolve readily in cold liquids. To make the syrup, heat equal parts sugar and water, stirring until the sugar has dissolved, then remove from the heat and let cool. You can sweeten the whole pitcher of tea with the syrup, or individual glasses can be sweetened. The simple syrup will keep in a tightly capped container in the refrigerator for up to a week.

THE ART OF TASTING TEA

Tasting is different from eating and drinking. The latter are done because of hunger or thirst. Tasting, in contrast, is a deliberate process in which sensory impressions are consciously identified and compared.

I like to use the example of music to explain this difference more fully. Both of my parents are extremely musical. My father was a professional singer, songwriter, trumpet player, and pianist for most of his life, and my mother was a piano instructor from the time I was a small child. They taught me how to listen to music in an intimate way so that I could appreciate its many different aspects. Is it a three-count or four-count piece? What is the beat? What is the tempo? When does the song change octaves? What is the mood of the music?

Drinking can be compared to background music that you hear while engaged in another activity. For example, do you realize that almost every television commercial includes music? Maybe you don't, because it is usually there only to create the right vibe for selling the product. Movies often have background music, too, to set the tone for a scene. But if the film is good, you are typically too engrossed in the story to pay attention to the music. Most hosts play music to set the mood for their party, but it is seldom the main event.

Tasting, however, can be compared to going to the symphony where music *is* the main event. Sitting in your seat waiting for the concert to start, you anticipate beginning. As the musicians walk onto the stage, you know you are in for a treat. Then the concert begins and you shut out the rest of your surroundings and listen intently. Each instrument is important to the overall beauty of the piece being played. You pay close attention as the violins start; then, as the brass instruments come in, you note the shift in the overall sound. You listen carefully to the beginning and ending of each piece, noting how these two elements set the work apart from others in the program. You think about how each piece makes you feel, how it affects your mood. This is what tasting is: it is slowing down and focusing on what your senses are telling you about what is in your mouth.

Wine lovers know there is a way to taste wine to enjoy it to its fullest. In fact, you have probably seen the ritual, or you may have even done it yourself. You pour the wine into a glass, check its color and opacity, swirl it to release its aroma, breathe in the fragrance, take a sip, and then roll the wine around in your mouth to expose it fully to your palate. Each step goes toward releasing the sensual taste of the grapes.

Just as there is a way to taste wine, there is way to taste tea, and the ritual is even more elaborate. Unlike wine, which comes fully prepared in a bottle, tea is processed to a certain point and then the tea drinker finishes the process through steeping. Although wine lovers cannot typically see, touch, or smell the grapes that were used to make the wine, a tea lover can do all three because he or she starts with the leaves, which adds to the overall enjoyment of tasting.

How and what we perceive as flavor depends directly on two of our senses, smell and taste.

But what we smell and taste is influenced by at least one other sense, sight. So, before you learn how to taste tea, you need to understand how the senses of sight, smell, and taste all come into play during the tea-tasting ritual.

You have undoubtedly heard the wisdom that we taste first with our eyes. I know that I am what some people call a tea geek, but I think tea leaves—both whole-leaf teas and broken-leaf teas—are beautiful, and an important part of tasting tea is enjoying their beauty. The tea master creates the shape of the leaf not only to ensure wonderful flavor and aroma but also to heighten its aesthetic value. When presented with hand-fashioned shapes, such as the delicate spheres of Jasmine Pearls, the flat, straight leaves of Dragon Well, or the semicurled leaves of Pi Luo Chun, it is difficult not to pause and appreciate the splendor. Some machine-processed teas are exquisite as well, such as the sticklike, rich green leaves of Japanese Sencha.

The color of the leaves is also pleasing to the eye. It is an indication of what type of tea you will taste and of the quality of the leaves. Do they have a gleam to them, a sign of freshness, or do they look dull, possibly indicating the tea is old?

Once you have looked at the leaves, the next sense that comes into play is that of smell. Most authorities agree that just a handful of detectable taste components exist, but when it comes to smell, we are much more sensitive. According to Janet A. Zimmerman, a culinary instructor and a staff writer at eGullet, an online service of the Society for Culinary Arts & Letters, the average person can identify thousands of different odors and about ten different intensities within each odor. That's because the olfactory receptors located on a small patch in the upper part of the nasal cavity are able to detect up to ten thousand unique odors. The best way to distinguish the aromas of any food or beverage, including tea, is to exhale with your mouth closed while the substance is in your mouth. I teach my students to exhale with their mouths closed after they have swallowed the tea as well. This is especially fun when tasting oolongs, which are known for their long finish. The students find it amazing that they can detect flavor through their nasal passages after the tea has been consumed.

Not being able to smell severely affects your ability to taste. You might have noticed this when you are congested. Temperature can also affect how a food or beverage smells. We detect more odors from substances when they are warm or hot than when they are cold. Think about how much stronger something smells when it is hot rather than cold. Garbage is a good, albeit not a pleasant, example. Most people know how much worse garbage smells on a hot summer day than in the chill of winter. Likewise, tea served hot will smell differently than tea served cold or iced.

Before we get to the sense of taste, we need to look at a closely related aspect of tasting known as mouthfeel, which is the sensation created by food or drink in the mouth. Different teas have different levels of astringency, which is what produces the dry, rough, puckery sensation in your mouth when you drink certain teas or red wines or eat unripe fruits. The astringency is caused by the presence of tannins, naturally occurring yellowish brown polyphenols (antioxidants) present in tea leaves. The higher the tannin content of a tea, the greater the astringency. One reason tea pairs so well with some foods is because its astringency refreshes the palate by sharply counterbalancing the foods, especially those high in fat. Simply put, it immediately reduces the "overlubrication" our mouths feel when we eat fatty foods. Mouthfeel can also detect the body or viscosity of a tea, that is, tell you how thick or thin it feels in your mouth.

The final sense is taste. The bumps on your tongue are called papillae. Inside some of those bumps are taste buds, which in turn contain taste receptors that signal the gustatory areas of your brain, allowing you to register a specific taste. Not everyone tastes the same things the same way, plus there is a genetic component to how strongly we taste things. All of this will come into play as you begin to taste tea. Don't worry if you don't have a strong sense of taste. It does not mean that you cannot enjoy tasting tea, but

Taste Sensitivity

Dr. Virginia Utermohlen-Lovelace of the Taste Science Laboratory, Cornell University, has done some brilliant research into how people taste things differently. In a interview I had with Dr. Utermohlen-Lovelace, she stated, "Taste sensitivity refers to the intensity with which you perceive tastes and flavors. People with high taste sensitivity experience tastes, and usually smells, too, as being very strong. They are also able to distinguish individual flavors in a mixture very well. For people with low taste sensitivity, tastes, smells, and flavors are not as strong and they come as a packaged deal."

Is one taste sensitivity level better than another? Dr. Utermohlen-Lovelace says no. Whether you have high taste sensitivity or low taste sensitivity does not make you more of an expert. It does, however, affect the choices you prefer.

rather that everyone's idea of how a tea tastes will vary. It may also be a good indication of why some people like certain teas better than others.

Just as temperature affects how a food or beverage smells, it also affects how it tastes. Bitter things taste less bitter when they are hot rather than at room temperature, while the perceived level of sweetness increases at cooler temperatures. This is good to remember when you taste

tea, since you are in control of the water temperature. At a tea tasting, it is sometimes fun to taste the same tea at different temperatures to see how the temperature alters the taste.

Now that you understand how important sight, aroma, mouthfeel, and taste are to your enjoyment of tea, you are ready to begin tasting. I have a memory bank of aromas and tastes that I draw on when I am tasting tea. This has allowed me to develop my own language to describe the many teas that I have tried over the years. Most people who have become serious tea drinkers rely on their own memory bank and a personalized language just as I do. So, as you begin to taste, reflect on the smells and tastes that you already know and try to apply them to the new experience of tasting tea. Be adventurous in your tasting and dig deeply into your memory bank, and soon both your memory bank and tea vocabulary will grow.

When I was working alongside a tea master in Taiwan, hand-processing Tung Ting oolong (see page 39, "Making Tung Ting Oolong"), orange blossoms kept coming to mind. As I inhaled the wonderful fragrance of the freshly plucked leaves and began to work with them, my memory bank kept taking me back to my childhood in southern Florida and the orchards of blooming orange trees. It was an unexpected sweet smell that I didn't know tea leaves could exude.

Understanding the Memory Bank of Smells

I have been told that I have a very strong sense of smell, and I must admit that others around me seldom smell things to the same degree that I do. This can be good or bad, of course, depending on the smell! Familiar scents can take me back to a time, place, person, or thing in my memory. When I smell someone wearing the cologne my father used to wear, for example, I am immediately returned to my childhood. It appears there is science to back this up.

According to the Taste Science Laboratory, which is part of the Division of Nutritional Sciences at Cornell University, smelling and memory are deeply connected. The laboratory's findings indicate that the olfactory nerve endings found in the roof of the nose when you smell or eat something alert the olfactory bulb to send smell messages to two critical parts of the brain, both located in the temporal lobe. The first part that is alerted is involved with memory, particularly memories of places. This explains why smells can evoke powerful memories of your experiences. The second part involves speech, and here the research has found that people smelling some scents can actually be inhibited from speaking or even thinking of words and are left with only visual thoughts. This second part also contains not only our emotional center but also our centers for evaluation, judgment, and decision making. So when someone reaches into his or her memory bank to characterize a smell or taste, many influences affect how that smell or taste is perceived.

Tasting Tea in Five Steps

It is a good idea to keep a journal as you begin tasting teas. It will help you establish a tea vocabulary to use as you reach into your memory bank, and it is a record of past tastings that can guide you in future purchases. You can also look back in your journal to see what specific tea leaves looked like and how fresh they appeared, and how long you infused them to create a cup you liked. Plus, if your tea purveyor runs out of a tea that you particularly like, you can review your tasting notes with the purveyor so that he or she can select a similar tea for you.

To appreciate the flavor of tea to its fullest, it is important to start with the leaf, which is easy whether you are steeping tea at home or at a tasting. As noted earlier, this gives tasting tea an advantage over tasting wine or even beer, because unless you have a home winery or brewery, the grapes or hops are not available.

1. **FIRST, LOOK AT THE DRY LEAVES.** What is their color? What is their shape? Are the leaves large or small? Are they full leaves or are they broken? Are they uniform? Do they appear fresh and have a good sheen? If you are keeping a journal, record some of your findings.

2. **NEXT, SMELL THE DRY LEAF.** Since the leaves release a stronger odor when they are heated, cup your hands over them and gently warm them by exhaling on them through your nose. This will heat them up so you can detect more aromas. What aroma is the leaf giving off? Can you compare it to something in your memory bank of smells? Note the smell in your journal so that later you can compare it with the smell of the infusion. This will help with future purchases, because usually all you can do when shopping is smell the dry leaf, and sometimes the scent of the dry leaf is much different from the flavor profile of the steeped infusion. This way the smell won't fool you!

3. **STEEP THE TEA.** Follow the instructions on page 61 ("How to Make Hot Tea") and be sure to save the wet leaves. Study a few of the wet leaves to see how they opened up during steeping. Did they open all the way? If not, this may indicate that another infusion is possible. How large are the leaves? How many leaves are joined together? Once they open, you can tell what was included in the pluck. Is it two leaves and a bud? Is it just leaves with no bud? Are they full leaves or broken? You cannot always detect from the dry leaves what was plucked because the leaves are twisted together from the rolling stage. If you paid for full-leaf tea, you want to make sure that is what you got. What is the color of the steeped leaf? Sometimes as the leaves infuse, the color isn't what you

The Role of the Professional Tea Taster

Most tea you drink has been tasted, or cupped (see page 79, "Professional Cupping"), by several different professional tea tasters before it reaches you. Tea is not a standardized product; it is an agricultural one. That means that each new crop does not necessarily taste the same as the previous one. This is when the professional tea taster goes to work.

The cupping of any tea begins with the farmer, whose harvest must be processed according to the specifications of the customer. Depending on the country of origin and the size of the farm, the farmer will either partially or fully process the leaves at an onsite facility or send them off to a factory for processing. Once the tea has been processed, the head of quality control—the tea taster—will taste the tea to determine if adjustments are necessary to achieve the best end product. His palate (tasters are traditionally men) will tell him what, if anything, needs to be done to improve the tea to satisfy the buyer, such as blending different batches together from different days or blending teas from surrounding tea fields. Professional tasters are like chefs creating a recipe. By tasting samples, they determine what the "tea recipe" may need in order meet the customer's expectations. But they must keep the price in mind at the same time. That means that, just like a chef who cannot add a bunch of expensive ingredients because the food costs will be too high, a taster cannot blend the most expensive teas together and still meet the price requirements of the buyer.

Large wholesale tea companies send their in-house tea buyers to countries of origin to cup teas they are interested in purchasing. A smaller wholesaler will hire a broker or a purveyor, also known as an agent, who cups teas in the country of origin for the company and then sends samples of the ones he thinks best meet what the company is looking for.

Once the samples are on hand, the wholesaler must taste them again. Tea is seasonal, which makes May through August the busiest cupping time. The samples are set up on a cupping table, the number of teas being tested usually limited by the size of the table, and the cupping begins. The first cupping focuses on elimination, that is, separating the acceptable teas from the unacceptable ones. Usually more than one taster cups the teas, so the tasters may compare notes as they work. The rejects are put aside and the acceptable samples are cupped again. The choices from this cupping are then usually sorted according to desired taste preferences and price. At this point, each tea is evaluated for price and the purchase price is negotiated and decided. The taster's objective is to get the very best tea he can at the best price for his customer. The tea is then on its way to the consumer.

expected. For example, steeped first flush Darjeeling leaves look like green tea leaves, even though they are the leaves of a black tea. Note as much as you can of these observations in your journal.

4. **NEXT, SMELL THE WET LEAF.** Does it give off a different odor than when it was dry? What do you smell, and can you relate it to something in your memory bank of smells? Then smell the steeped tea, breathing in deeply as you do. What does it smell like? Does it smell similar to the dry and wet leaf or is it surprisingly different?

5. **FINALLY, TASTE THE TEA.** If you are in a place where you can slurp without being regarded as rude, give the tea a good slurp along with a lot of air. This allows the tea to penetrate all the different parts of your tongue and palate for the fullest flavor. What do you taste? What is the mouthfeel of the tea? Is it drying on your tongue, which would indicate the astringency level of the tea? What is the viscosity; that is, does it feel thick or thin? Does it have a natural sweetness? What is the finish of the tea and the aftertaste? Can you draw on your memory bank to come up with good descriptions? Does the tea have a long finish; that is, does the flavor remain strong after the tea is swallowed? Again, record your findings in your journal, as these notes will help you

in the future with pairing teas, cooking with tea, or making tea cocktails, all of which are discussed in chapter four.

I hope this helps you to appreciate fine tea on a whole new level. When I think about how much goes into making a cup of tea, from the farmer who tended the plant and the people who processed the leaves to the wholesaler who evaluated and then bought the tea and the retail shop that chose to carry it, I can see it only as a truly special beverage.

Ideas for Tea Tastings

If you find yourself wanting to do more with tea than just drink it for pure enjoyment, you can put together a tasting, either for yourself or a group. You will need to purchase a digital metric scale and one or more professional cupping sets. A cupping set is what professional tea tasters use to evaluate tea. It is made of white porcelain and consists of three parts: a steeping cup that has a small ridge opening on one side, a lid that fits over the steeping cup, and a bowl. If you've decided to host a tasting, you'll probably need eight to ten sets. You will also need a spoon for each taster, or if you don't want folks using a dirty spoon with each new tea, you will need a set of clean spoons for each tea.

To cup teas, you need to weigh 2 to 3 grams of tea for each taster and put them into the steeping cup of the cupping set. Professional cuppers use boiling water no matter what class of tea is being tasted, but this might be a bit much for novices. I advise starting off with the water temperatures suggested in the steeping chart on page 64. Decide on a steeping time and be consistent with that, too. Pour the water over the leaves and place the lid on top. When the allotted time has finished, the tasters decant their tea into the bowl with the lid still on the cup part of the set. Then, before they try the tea, they should carefully lift the lid off the steeping cup and smell the infused leaves. Keeping the leaves covered in such a small space will heighten their aroma.

If you don't want to purchase cupping sets, you can use white teacups, all in the same size and style. You will have to use an infuser with each cup and have a separate saucer to put the leaves on when they are done steeping.

Once you have assembled the equipment, you will need to choose the teas and then put them in the order in which they will be tasted. White, green, yellow, oolong, black, and finally dark is a good way to proceed, as it is difficult to grasp the flavor notes in a delicate white tea once you have tasted a bold black tea. If you will not be tasting all of the tea classes, start with the lightest tea and work your way down to the darkest. Be sure to have glasses of water and some unsalted plain crackers on hand to cleanse palates between teas.

I find that a tasting is the best way to compare teas in order to figure out which ones I like best. When you drink them side by side, you are better able to detect the differences. I do the same thing when I am comparing foods.

Even if you are the only participant for the tea tasting, it is important to settle on an organizing principle. There are countless ways to put together a tasting. Here are some ideas to get you started:

- Include an example from each class of tea, white, green, yellow, oolong, black, and dark. This is a great introduction for beginners.

- Choose a country and feature the same type of tea from different regions within that country.
    - Black teas of India from Nilgiri, Assam, and Darjeeling.
    - Oolong teas of Taiwan from different growing regions.
    - Ceylon (Sri Lanka) grown in low, middle, and high elevations.

- Choose the classic teas from China, such as Silver Needle white tea, Dragon Well green tea, Tie Guanyin oolong, Keemun black, and Pu'erh.

- Choose green teas from China.

- Choose oolong teas from China.

- Choose black teas from China.

- Choose white teas from China.

- Choose classic green teas from Japan.

- Host a Pu'erh tasting, with Sheng Pu'erh (uncooked, or green type) and Shou Pu'erh (cooked, or black type) of different ages.

- Choose the teas of South Korea.

- Choose green teas from around the world.

- Choose black teas from around the world.

- Choose white teas from around the world.

- Compare oolongs from China and Taiwan.

- Choose the same type of tea but of differing grades of quality. You may discover that you don't prefer what is considered the highest quality!

- Choose different blends, such as English Breakfast and Irish Breakfast.

- Choose teas of Africa, such as teas from Kenya, Rwanda, Tanzania, and Malawi.

- Host a blind tasting and let your guests try to guess what they are tasting.

As you can see, you are limited only by your own imagination. Be daring, be bold, and most important, have fun. You might even enjoy tasting tea as part of a tea ceremony, which is explored in chapter three.

Professional Cupping

Professional cupping is more elaborate than what happens at your tea tastings, even if you use cupping sets. First, the tea is carefully weighed and put into the steeping cup. The taster looks at the leaves carefully and then warms them by exhaling on them through his nostrils (as noted earlier, most professional cuppers are male). Some tasters bury their nose right in the leaves, heat them up by gently exhaling out of their nose, and then breathe in deeply. Before they move on to the next sample, they blow their nose to rid it any trapped leaf bits that may compromise their judgment. Some of the best tasters can often tell how good a tea will be by completing just these two steps of looking at it and smelling it.

Next, boiling water is poured over the leaves, the lid is placed on the cup, and a timer is set for the preferred steeping time, usually between four and five minutes. Boiling water and the same steeping time are used for all classes of tea. When the time is up, the tea, or liquor, in the still-covered steeping cup is thoroughly drained into the cupping bowl.

Before tasting the tea, the taster lifts the lid and smells the freshly steeped leaves. Their fragrance, which is potent because it has been trapped in the covered cup, can give the taster a good indication of the quality of the tea. The cup and lid are then turned upside down so the wet leaves pile up on the lid. The steeping cup is lifted off, turned upright, and the lid, with the leaves, is set on top. Once again, the taster evaluates the look and smell of the leaves.

The tea is now finally tasted. The taster dips a spoon into the tea, brings it to his mouth, and slurps the tea along with large amounts of air, which sprays the tea all over the tongue and the palate. This ensures that not only all of the taste sensors but also the nasal passages are involved.

The tea is never swallowed, as swallowing it is thought to dull the taste buds, thus impairing the taster's sensitivity. Once the tea has fully circulated around the mouth, it is discharged into a spittoon. The spitting of tea is an art form in itself, and it is important that it be done properly. Usually only one spittoon is shared among several tasters, which means that they must be careful that the velocity at which the spit leaves their mouth—a talent that requires mastering both puckering the lips and using the tongue to direct the discharge—is great enough to land it in the receptacle, rather than on their chin or the floor. Then, before moving to the next sample, the taster makes notes, carefully describing the leaf, the liquor of the leaf, the taste, and the aftertaste.

CHAPTER THREE

TEA CEREMONIES AND RITUALS

Experiencing Tea in Many Different Ways

A tea ceremony is a prescribed way of making
and serving tea. Depending on where you are
in the world, it can be highly structured, simple
and understated, or somewhere in between.
Some gatherings focus on the making and
serving of the tea; others seem more concerned
with the tea things—pots, cups, pitchers,
bowls—the accompanying savories and sweets,
and who is attending. Dozens of interesting
tea ceremonies are held around the world,
some to celebrate an occasion, others as a
demonstration of respect and hospitality, and
still others as a solitary cup to aid meditation.
I am including some of my favorites in this
chapter, beginning with the Chinese tea
ceremony that started it all.

CHINESE TEA CEREMONY

Temple monks were the first to organize a ceremony surrounding tea drinking in China. It was a simple ritual designed to teach respect for nature, to express humility, and to achieve an overall sense of peace. The more elevated Chinese tea ceremony dates back to the Tang dynasty (618–907), when it was primarily enjoyed by the elite. In *The Classic of Tea*, written between 760 and 780, the famed Chinese poet and scholar Lu Yu describes a ceremony that required nearly thirty pieces of equipment and probably almost as many servants. By the time of the Ming dynasty (1368–1644), tea drinking had spread down through the classes, along with a more manageable ceremony.

Nowadays, the Chinese ceremony is most commonly called *gongfu cha*, and most of its customs are believed to date to the last years of the Ming dynasty. Its spirit is described as *he, jing, yi, zhen,* which translates to "peace, quiet, enjoyment, truth." The Chinese view this ceremony—this making and serving of tea—as an art form, using the term *cha yi*, or the "art of tea," to describe it. That description becomes clear when you translate *gongfu* (sometimes spelled *kung fu*), which means "skill from practice" or "patient effort," a phrase that can be applied to mastering any

art form, from the martial arts to the culinary arts. In the context of tea, *gongfu cha* essentially means "patient effort tea ceremony" or "skill from practice tea ceremony," and while you don't have to be an expert to begin experimenting with it, the idea is that you will learn the ceremony by practicing it.

I am far from an expert in *gongfu cha*, but I have watched the ceremony many times and have participated in it on occasion. One of my fondest memories of *gongfu cha* is from my time in Taiwan, where I went with a group of friends to a small teahouse. We each ordered a different kind of tea and spent the entire afternoon taking turns making tea for one another. Even though none of us was an expert, we all enjoyed practicing our art form while talking, sharing, and laughing the afternoon away. Although our

Tea or Cha?

Why two different names for the same beverage? There is one Chinese ideogram for tea. But because of the many regional language varieties, or dialects, in China, its pronunciation varies from place to place. In some parts of China, it was called *cha* or some variation of the term, and in others it was called some variation on the word *tea*. Those names spread and took hold in different languages around the world, and today both words are used for the same beverage.

outing was a much more informal occasion of *gongfu cha*, the essence of "skill from practice" was used as we each tried our hand at making tea, and our "patient effort" was exercised as we waited for each infusion of all the different kinds of tea we tried that day.

Chinese tea ceremonies are more about the tea than the technique. According to Chinese tea aficionado Dan Robertson of the Tea House, "The tea's *si, xiang, wei, xing,* which translates to 'color, aroma, flavor, and shape,' should be appreciated. The various steps in the ceremony accentuate these qualities. They also serve to bring a sense of formality and politeness to the experience. Both host and guest have their roles. The environment should be clean and serene. The host is obligated to make [his or her] guests feel comfortable. Thoughtful discussion of inconsequential things is encouraged and talk of important matters is not entertained."

The Chinese ceremony has evolved over time, with different kinds of tea being used and different levels of formality being enforced, but the spirit of the ritual remains the same. I am going to describe what I believe to be the most popular way *gongfu cha* is enjoyed, using oolong tea. Throughout the ceremony, it is important to keep movements graceful and always to serve in a circular motion. For more formal ceremonies, always serve with your right hand in counter-clockwise motion

as to be welcoming the participants into the ceremony. For less formal ceremonies, left-handed people may use their left hand for serving except change to a clockwise circular motion to make all guests feel welcome.

The tea is typically brewed in a small Eastern-style teapot. Although you may use any kind of small teapot, a Yixing teapot, which is an unglazed pot made in the Yixing area, near Shanghai in Jiangsu Province, from the local clay, is traditional. Some tea experts consider these the best vessels for brewing oolongs and Pu'erhs. Because the pot is unglazed, the clay absorbs the flavor of the tea every time it is used for brewing. This enhances the flavor of the tea, but it also means that you must reserve the pot for brewing only one type of tea. Authentic Yixing teapots can be quite pricey, so you may want to look for less costly unglazed pots, which will work as well. The other equipment you will need for brewing includes the following:

- Set of small (thimble-size) teacups
- Tea drip tray (two-level tray, with a perforated top level for drainage) or a wide, shallow heat-proof bowl
- Kettle of water heated to around 195°F/90°C for oolong
- Waste-water bowl
- Tea scoop or teaspoon
- Caddy of loose-leaf tea

- Tea towel
- Optional set of smelling cups (see "Smelling Cups," right)
- Optional tea utensils, such as bamboo tongs and a curved bamboo stick
- Optional pitcher
- Optional tea plates or saucers for serving cups to guests

Conducting the Ceremony

1. **HEATING THE EQUIPMENT.** Place the teapot and the teacups (and smelling cups, if using) on the tea drip tray. Carefully fill the teapot with hot water from the kettle. Put the lid on the teapot and pour a little hot water over the teapot to warm the outside. Next, fill all the cups (and smelling cups, if using) with hot water for just a moment or two to heat them. Then empty the teapot and the cups into the waste-water bowl or the drain on the tea tray.

2. **FILLING THE TEAPOT.** Using the tea scoop, reach into the tea caddy and fill the scoop with tea leaves. (You can instead use bamboo tongs, if you have them.) Fill the teapot roughly one-third to two-thirds full of tea. This may seem like a lot, but the tea will be steeped for several infusions. You may need to experiment with how full to fill the teapot

Smelling Cups

Also called "fragrance cups" or "aroma cups," smelling cups are sometimes used when serving tea, especially teas like oolongs that are known for their alluring fragrance. They are specifically made to go with the thimble-size teacups that are used with Eastern-style teapots. A smelling cup is designed to fit inside a small teacup, which is sometimes referred to as its partner. The smelling cup is tall and slender, a shape that helps trap the fragrance of the tea. The Chinese have a name for when the empty teacup is placed over the smelling cup and before the cups are inverted. They call it "happy family."

for your taste. It is nice to offer your guests an opportunity to smell the dry leaves that have been placed in the heated teapot, as the heat from the pot accentuates their lovely aroma.

3. **WASHING AND WAKING UP THE LEAVES.** Pour the hot water over the leaves in the teapot, place the lid on top, and pour hot water over the top of the teapot as well. Allow the leaves to steep for 15 to 30 seconds, then pour off the liquid into the wastewater bowl or tray drain. This infusion is not meant to be consumed. It is a purely ceremonial act, in which the leaves are washed and allowed to come alive, so to speak.

4. **FIRST INFUSION FOR DRINKING.** Once again, pour the hot water over the tea leaves in the teapot and place the lid on top, then pour hot water over the top of the teapot. Allow the leaves to steep for 15 to 30 seconds. If you will be pouring directly from the pot into the cups, use the tea towel to dry off the bottom of the pot. If you will be using a pitcher to serve the tea, pour the tea into the pitcher. By decanting the tea into the pitcher, you ensure that all the tea is the same strength, which means as you serve the tea, you can fill each cup to the top, rather than moving back and forth among them as you do when using a pot.

If you are using the pot to serve, do not fill the teacups one at a time. Instead, pour just a little tea into each one before going on to the next one, moving among all the cups in a circular motion. This ensures that the tea in each cup is the same strength. Once you have poured nearly all of the tea, shake out one last drop into each cup, which the Chinese believe is the best tea in the pot. They call these last drops *Han Xin dian bing*, or "Han Xin counts his troops." It refers to the fact that General Han Xin, who died late in the third century B.C.E., never lost a battle and never left any of his troops behind idling and getting bitter, which is why you must never leave the last drops in the teapot. If you have tea plates, place the cups on them.

If you are using smelling cups, fill them a little at a time as well, moving back and forth among them. They should be no more than three-fourths full when the last drops are added. (This is true if using a pitcher as well, though you can fill them one at a time.) Then invert a teacup on top of each smelling cup and quickly invert them together, so that all the liquid flows into the teacup. If you have tea plates, place each pair of inverted cups on a plate and offer a plate to each guest. Serve yourself last. Each person uses a slow twisting motion to lift the smelling cup off of the teacup, and then everyone rolls the smelling cup between the palms of both hands while inhaling the lovely fragrance in it left behind by the tea. Rolling the cup in your palms not only releases the fragrance but also warms your hands and gently massages their pressure points, relieving stress and tension.

5. **DRINKING THE FIRST INFUSION.** To hold the teacup properly, use the thumb and the middle finger of your dominant hand. Sometimes women use the middle finger of their opposite hand to support the bottom of the cup. Turn the cup at about a ninety-degree angle in toward your body. Bring the cup to your nose and enjoy the fragrance of the

tea. The cups are small and the tea is meant to be drunk in three sips. The first sip is to enjoy the fragrance of the tea. Move the tea around in your mouth to draw as much from it as possible. The second sip is to enjoy the taste of the tea, which means that you must bathe your tongue with it. The third sip finishes the tea in the cup. While the tea is in your mouth, breathe out to enjoy the flavor more fully. Then after you swallow, breathe out again with your mouth closed to enjoy the tea's wonderful lingering finish.

6. **DRINKING SUBSEQUENT INFUSIONS.** Steps 4 and 5 can be repeated for as long as the tea leaves give up flavor, taking note of how each infusion tastes and smells differently than the others. A fine oolong should give anywhere from three to six infusions. For each subsequent infusion, add 15 to 30 seconds to the infusion time. Fresh water may need to be heated for these additional infusions.

Here are some additional tips and suggestions for conducting a *gongfu cha*:

- A newly purchased unglazed earthenware teapot must be "seasoned" before it can be used the first time. Place it in a saucepan and fill the pan with the kind of brewed tea that you plan to brew in the pot. Bring the tea to a gentle boil and then turn off the heat and leave the pot to soak in the tea for 5 to 6 hours.

- If any tea remains from an infusion, pour it out of the pot into the waste-water bowl so that a fresh infusion is made every time.

- If tea leaves get stuck in the spout of the teapot, the best tool to dislodge them is a curved bamboo stick.

- When cleaning your unglazed teapot, be sure to remove all of the tea leaves. If you have bamboo tongs, you can use them to get the leaves out of the pot. Then rinse the teapot with water and allow it to air-dry. Never use soap to clean it.

- If you decide also to include black or Pu'erh tea or both in the ceremony, be sure to use a different pot for each type of tea. The class of tea and the teapot become one. Some tea enthusiasts say that you can make tea just by adding hot water to a Yixing teapot that has been used for many years.

- Use the tea towel at any point during the ceremony to dry off the bottom of the teapot or the teacups.

- The tea ceremony should be a relaxed time. Each motion should be slow, graceful, and purposeful. Never hurry the process.

Chinese Wedding Tea Ceremony

For a traditional Chinese wedding, the couple holds two tea ceremonies to show respect for their parents and their heritage. On the morning of the wedding day, the bride serves tea to her parents in their home to thank them for raising her. Then, on either the day of the wedding or the day after, the newlyweds serve tea to the groom's parents and relatives, typically kneeling in front of them. In response to this gesture, the couple receives lucky red envelopes, known as *hongbao* in Mandarin and *lai see* in Cantonese, filled with money or sometimes jewelry.

If you are a bride or groom, performing a tea ceremony for your parents and grandparents before your wedding to show your gratitude is a thoughtful gesture, even if you are not Chinese. Make it your own ceremony—you do not need to include the red packets, for example—one that your family will remember.

JAPANESE TEA CEREMONY

In Japan, the tea ceremony is commonly called *chanoyu*, literally, "hot water for tea." Even though the phrase implies simplicity, the ceremony itself is far from that. It is the most ritualized way of serving and drinking tea practiced anywhere in the world. Some people study this formal procedure for decades, and even most teachers have teachers, because of the numerous levels of certification that an instructor can acquire.

A second term exists within *chanoyu* that perhaps better describes the intricacy of the ritual. It is *chado*, which translates to "the way of tea" or "the path of tea." It was adopted from the Chinese term *cha dao* by Japanese monks after visiting China in the ninth century. On their return, they took what they learned about *cha dao* and blended it with many things in their own culture, to produce what is now studied and practiced as *chado*. *Chanoyu* is one of the most highly structured ways in which *chado* can be expressed.

Tea master Sen no Rikyu (1522–91), who is known as the Saint of the Tea Ceremony, is credited with creating the guidelines and beliefs of the ceremony, many of them deeply rooted in Buddhism, Shintoism, and Confucianism. The ceremony is regarded as more than just a system of etiquette. It is practiced as a mental discipline that helps cultivate wisdom. The philosophy, which applies to both the host and the guests, is based on *wa*, *kei*, *sei*, and *jaku*, which translate to "harmony," "respect," "purity," and "tranquility."

- **HARMONY** (*wa*) can be achieved between self and another and between self and an object by attaining balance.

- **RESPECT** (*kei*) is granted to all, regardless of status or other social distinctions by a love for all.

- **PURITY** (*sei*) of the spirit is essential and is symbolized by cleaning yourself, the tearoom, and the tea equipment.

- **TRANQUILITY** (*jaku*) is attained through the embodiment of harmony, respect, and purity.

Rikyu used the tea ceremony as a parable for how people should live their lives and maintain relationships with others. He outlined seven principles to guide people in the way of tea and thus in everyday life, each of which can be mastered only if one exercises great discipline:

1. Put your heart into making tea and place emphasis not on the etiquette of preparing tea or the utensils used but rather on serving tea that your guest will enjoy.

2. Prepare charcoal in a way that creates fire to boil water quickly but not wastefully.

3. Arrange the flowers so as to bring out their unadorned beauty as it would be in nature.

4. Keep the tearoom cool in the summer and warm in the winter.

5. Be ahead of time to give yourself the comfort of not doing everything at the last moment.

6. Prepare an umbrella even when it is not expected to rain, because one should always be prepared for unexpected events.

7. Realize the importance of being considerate to others and do things with others in mind, rather than yourself.

Another underlying philosophy of *chanoyu* is the idea that no two ceremonies are alike. Each cup of tea and each teatime will differ from any other because of differences in tea, the people you are with, and the atmosphere of the space in which you have gathered. The beautiful Japanese phrase for this is *ichigo-ichie*, which translates as "one meeting, one time." This principle applies to life as well. Each moment is unique and will never be again. It should be appreciated and viewed as precious.

A Japanese tea ceremony can be held for a variety of reasons, such as to acknowledge a special occasion or to welcome a new season. Traditionally, the space includes seasonal flowers in a simple arrangement (*chanoyu* has its own style of flower arrangement known as *chabana*) and a hanging scroll displaying calligraphy that reflects the season and the occasion.

The utensils for the ceremony play a large part in the overall ritual. They are made of various materials—ceramic, different metals, bamboo, straw, cane—and are chosen for their suitability to the occasion and the season of the year. They are not supposed to match but rather to be in harmony with one another, known as *suki*, or "refined rusticity." *Chanoyu* involves a lot of paraphernalia. Here is a list of the basic equipment:

- *Chawan* (tea bowl)
- *Chasen* (bamboo tea whisk)
- *Chashaku* (bamboo, wood, or ivory tea scoop)
- *Kama* (kettle, usually made of cast iron)
- *Hishaku* (bamboo water ladle)
- *Mizusashi* (cold-water container)
- *Kensui* (waste-water container, for rinsing tea bowls)
- *Chakin* (white cotton or linen cloth, for wiping tea bowls clean after use)
- *Chatsubo* (ceramic tea storage jar)
- *Fukusa* (colored silk cloth, for cleaning and for handling hot *kama* lid)

The ceremony is traditionally conducted in a teahouse, or *chashitsu*, that has a garden attached on one side. The structure is simple and the interior has a restful atmosphere—an environment that ensures that everyone will feel tranquil in it. The ceremony will differ depending on the occasion, the level of formality, the season, the time of day, and other factors. For example, some ceremonies include a meal, which is then followed by the tea service. The proper service of the tea is intricate and the details surrounding it are numerous. One of the simplest Japanese tea ceremonies, though certainly not a lesser one, is known as *usucha*, or "thin tea." Here are the basic elements of this ceremony:

1. The guests arrive by walking through a garden and then proceed to the next step in an order predetermined in advance by the host.

2. In the garden, the guests "purify" their hands and mouth with water from a basin.

3. The guests remove their footwear and enter the tearoom through a small door that naturally makes them bow, which is a sign of respect.

4. At this point, guests should take time to notice the wall hanging, the floral arrangement, and the various tea-related wares and accessories.

5. Each guest sits in a kneeling position on the *tatami* (straw) mats that cover the floor, with the seating arrangement specified by the host.

6. When the host enters the tearoom, formal greetings are exchanged.

7. Each guest is offered a small sweet known as a *kashi*, which he or she sets close by in the proper place for future enjoyment.

8. The host goes out of the tearoom and returns with the tea bowls in which he or she will start making the tea. No conversation is allowed.

9. The host then signals the guests to relax, and at this point, the guests begin to eat the reserved sweet and conversation is allowed.

10. The host makes the Matcha and serves a bowl of tea to each guest, who then drinks the tea.

11. Guests appreciate the artistry of the bowls in silence.

12. The host cleans the bowls and utensils and everyone is still silent.

13. The host returns to the kitchen for fresh water for the next occasion, whether or not more guests are expected.

14. Closing salutations are exchanged.

If you are invited to attend a *chanoyu*, here are several rules of etiquette to keep in mind:

- If you accept the invitation, you must not cancel later, as your acceptance is viewed as a commitment.

- Let the host know if this is your first time at a *chanoyu*.

- Arrive early.

- You will be seated on the floor and will most likely be kneeling, so dress appropriately.

- Bring with you a folded tissue (*kaishi*), a cake pick (*kuromoji*), and a folding fan (*sensu*).

- Be sure to drink the entire portion of tea and eat everything you are served.

- Each tea implement used in a tea gathering (including the scroll, flowers, and food) has been thoughtfully selected by your host and has special meaning. They should be treated with appreciation. Admire them and compliment your host with sincerity.

- Two or three days after the ceremony, call or write a note to express your appreciation for the invitation. This is known as *korei* or "thanking afterward."

I remember being mesmerized the first time I watched a Japanese tea ceremony being conducted. It was so serene, restful, and completely different from what I had ever seen. My friend

How to Prepare Matcha

Matcha, a green tea in which the leaves have been ground to a fine powder, is at the center of the Japanese tea ceremony. To make it, you will need a tea bowl, a fine-mesh strainer, a bamboo whisk, and a tea scoop. Here are the basic instructions for each cup:

1. Measure 1½ to 2 teaspoons Matcha.

2. Set the strainer over the bowl and gently sift the tea through the strainer into the bowl. This keeps the tea from clumping and helps to achieve a nice foam on the top.

3. Pour about ⅓ cup/75 ml hot water (about 165°F/74°C) over the tea.

4. Begin whisking the tea briskly back and forth in the bowl. When foam begins to develop, slowly lift the whisk from the bowl and enjoy the tea.

Donna Fellman, an author, tea specialist, and educator, told me that the first time she witnessed it she was so entranced by the beauty and peacefulness of it that she was "moved to tears." Donna went on to study *chanoyu* for more than a dozen years.

You may wonder why someone would spend so much time studying this tea ceremony. Various reasons exist for the length of study, some of which have to do with the countless variations on the ceremony itself, the many utensils used, and the difficulty in achieving an understanding of certain aspects of Japanese culture, including its language. People who study the ceremony for long periods often have reasons for doing so other than learning its many intricacies. Donna loved the way it made her feel and loved being in the tearoom. Another friend, tea specialist and speaker Judith Krall-Russo, who has studied *chanoyu* for more than nine years, says she relishes being in the moment, of having no idea what time it is. For her, it is as if "time just dissolves."

Others might be curious why you can't just read a book and then begin to practice *chanoyu*. Donna equates the situation to that of being a painter. "An artist can buy paints and a canvas and begin to paint," she explains. "If the artist really wants to learn painting techniques, however, he or she needs a teacher. It is the same with the Japanese tea ceremony."

Many of the things that you learn as you study the tea ceremony influence everyday life. Judith told me she began by signing up for a ten-week course so that she could teach a simple program on the ceremony. She extended her study for a very different reason, however. "For me now," she explained, "it is a lesson in mindfulness that carries over into my everyday life. I find that I am more temperate and I have learned to be more aware and appreciative of what I have and what is around me." Although the ceremony is rooted in Zen Buddhism, you don't have to be a Buddhist to practice it. Everyone can benefit from learning to be more aware and mindful. For some, the way of tea becomes a way of life. I think Donna summed it up best by saying, "All that I learned from *chanoyu* is in my cup."

TAIWANESE TEA CEREMONY

If you want to experience a more informal Asian tea ceremony where you may feel less intimidated about how to make and serve tea, look to the Taiwanese ceremony known as *wu-wo*. This is a fairly new ceremony, created in 1990 by Grand Master Tsai Rong Tsang, director of the Lu-Yu Tea Culture Institute in Taipei. A part of what the institute does is educate tea drinkers in Taiwan and beyond about the various methods and techniques of Chinese tea culture. Toward that end, a large *wu-wo* tea ceremony is held every two years in a different country—since 1990, China, South Korea, Japan, Singapore, and the United States have hosted the event—or a region in Taiwan.

This ritual was created to encourage all people regardless of tea expertise, age, sex, nationality, or wealth to participate. Taking a close look into the meaning of *wu-wo* explains more. The Chinese word *wu* means "void" or "absolute emptiness" with regard to the mind or senses, and *wo* means "mine," "self," or "being." When these two words are linked, they express a beautiful thought: Empty your mind of any pretense or thoughts and free yourself of any physical or mental attachments. This puts every participant on the same level, which is what makes this tea ritual perfect for everyone.

The ceremony works best with a group of at least four people participating and some spectators watching. The group sits in a circle on mats, cushions, or stools. If the group is large, two circles are formed. The spectators sit or stand around the outside of the circle(s). According to Steven R. Jones, a certified international *wu-wo* tea master instructor, the ceremony is governed by seven principles:

1. Seating is random. There is no priority seating regardless of social status.

2. Each participant serves his or her rounds of brewed tea in the same direction, so that the service is done smoothly, and no reward, such as a thank-you, is expected, because everyone must remain silent.

3. Participants accept and appreciate different teas. There is no bias.

4. Participants brew the tea the best they can, always concentrating on improving.

5. The ceremony has no director. Everyone follows public announcements.

6. Everyone remains silent during brewing to cooperate and appear in group rhythm and harmony.

7. No one is confined to brewing tea in a specific manner. Thus, no distinction is made among tea schools or regions.

Each participant needs to bring the following:

- Teapot
- Hot water in a thermos with a capacity four times greater than your teapot
- Tea for brewing at least four pots
- Four teacups and four disposable cups
- Tea tray
- Tea pitcher
- Watch or timer for brewing
- Small cloth for cleaning
- Mat, stool, or cushion to sit on
- Tarp, cloth, or towel on which to put the tea-brewing setup
- Cloth wraps for teaware and a basket, backpack, or bag for toting the ware

Once a circle of participants has formed, a "teaware appreciation and friendship time" is held. This is when people get to know one another and take the opportunity to admire the different tea setups that everyone has brought. It is also the only time allowed for talking, as the participants must remain silent during the rest of the ceremony. After this relatively brief time, the participants return to their tea setups and get ready to brew. A person who has been selected in advance and is not part of the circle will make public announcements that will direct each participant on how to serve his or her brewed tea. This will be the only person talking for the balance of the ritual. Here is how the tea ceremony is performed:

1. A public announcement will instruct you to brew your first pot of tea. When the tea is ready, pour it into four cups. Put three teacups on your tray and serve them to the three participants immediately to your left, saving the fourth cup for yourself. If the participant to whom you are serving a cup is still seated, you should bow to each other without speaking.

2. When you are done serving, return to your place. There should be three cups of tea served to you as well. Once everyone has finished serving and is seated again, the tasting of the tea can begin. Again, all of this is done silently.

3. When everyone is done tasting the first round of tea, a public announcement will instruct participants to brew a second pot. This infusion is poured into the disposable cups and is served silently to four spectators. After serving, you return again to your seat.

4. Now you brew your third pot of tea and pour it into a pitcher. You then stand up and pour tea from the pitcher for the same participants you served with your first pot, using the same cups, which are still at their place in front of each participant. After you have finished serving, return to your seat and pour some tea for yourself. After everyone has finished serving, enjoy the tea that has been served to you and the tea you have poured for yourself.

5. After the third brew, sometimes 3 to 5 minutes are set aside for music or meditation, known as "post–tea drinking activity." This allows the participants to reflect on what they have just experienced.

6. To conclude, the participants gather their cups, clean them, and pack up everything they brought with them. When everything is stowed, the tea ceremony is over.

My first experience with this type of tea ceremony was at a tea trade conference in 2012. All of the participants were in some facet of the tea business, which made it especially fascinating to watch. I decided not to participate so that I could grasp the ceremony more fully. As I observed the large group of some fifty people, many of whom were my friends and colleagues, I was moved by the lack of hierarchy in the ceremony. Some of the participants were highly accomplished purveyors in the specialty tea world, others were their good customers, and still others were just getting started in the tea industry. Despite the wide range of status, everyone was focused on making the best pot of tea possible for others to enjoy. As I watched, I saw how the imposed silence of the ceremony ensured that the group experienced a harmonious exchange.

ENGLISH TEA CEREMONIES

As noted in chapter one, it was not until Portugal's Catherine of Braganza married Charles II that tea drinking came into vogue in England. The marriage, arranged partially to help pay off the many debts of the king, came with a large dowry that included tea. According to some reports, the first thing the soon-to-be queen asked for as she disembarked from the ship that had carried her to her new home in May 1662 was a cup of tea. Tea drinking soon became fashionable and spread from the ladies of the court to the aristocracy to the upper class. By 1700, tea was being served in hundreds of coffeehouses to folks of more modest means. Its growing popularity prompted the government to tax it, which in turn created a big business in tea smuggling. In 1784, the government, in an effort to curb crime, dramatically reduced the tax on tea, which quickly made smuggling unprofitable.

Mealtimes were evolving along with tea consumption. By the 1800s, on a typical day, breakfast was served between eight and nine o'clock in the morning and the main meal was served at half past seven or later in the evening. This left a large gap in the day without sustenance, so a newly created light meal became commonplace. It was known variously as luncheon, nuncheon, or as Jane Austen liked to call it in her stories, noonshine. With lunch being a light meal and dinner still six or more hours away, what we now know as afternoon tea came into fashion.

Afternoon Tea

Although Anna Maria Russell, the seventh duchess of Bedford, is credited with "inventing" afternoon tea in 1841, it is believed that many others were already sitting down to tea in the afternoon when the duchess came up with the idea. As the story goes, Anna had asked that tea and something to eat (probably some bread and butter) be brought to her bedroom because she was experiencing a sinking feeling (most likely hunger pains). She soon began to invite friends to share in her afternoon repast of tea and snacks.

Afternoon tea was also known as "low tea" because guests were comfortably seated in low armchairs and the tea was served on side tables or coffee tables. The idea spread through the upper and middle classes as a way for women to entertain their friends and gossip. The meal soon grew a bit grander and often included crustless finger sandwiches, scones, and desserts. Those without great means in the middle class still managed to have afternoon tea, but they would do it potluck-style to conserve funds, a good idea for afternoon tea even today if your budget is limited.

Taking tea in the afternoon is unquestionably a luxury. As with other tea ceremonies in this chapter, it allows you to slow down, spend quality time with family and friends, and enjoy good tea and food. It is also a wonderful way to celebrate an impending wedding, birth, or other celebratory event. When our children were young, my husband and I began a tradition of taking them out for afternoon tea around Christmastime. We all continue to look forward to it every year, even though our kids are now much older. When they were little, they loved the idea of going to a fancy place and eating with their fingers. They now enjoy it because it has become a tradition. It also is a great way to spend family time together during a busy season of the year. My husband sometimes treats me to an afternoon tea out. We spend the whole time drinking tea, eating, and talking uninterrupted, pausing only when the occasional new teapot is brought to the table.

To serve an afternoon tea in your home doesn't mean you have to have all matching china and a fabulous silver service. You can make it as formal or informal as you like. It is centered more on etiquette and manners than some other tea ceremonies are, but that should not discourage you. For the tea itself, you will need a teapot, a sugar bowl and a cream pitcher, a plate for lemon slices, cups and saucers, teaspoons, and utensils for ferrying the sugar and lemon slices to the cups. For the food service, you will usually need small plates, knives or spreaders, and forks. Whether you go out or stay home, here are some suggestions to make your afternoon tea enjoyable.

Tips for Tea Drinking

- If you are entertaining at home, ask someone to pour the tea for your other guests. It is an honor to be asked.

- Fill the cups three-fourths full to allow guests room for adding milk and also to reduce the risk of spillage.

- If you add sugar and milk to your tea, I suggest pouring the tea, putting the sugar in the tea, and then adding the milk. If you are using milk only, pour the tea into the cup and then pour in the milk. That said, this order is still under discussion by those who debate the rules of tea etiquette.

- Offer small, thin lemon slices, never wedges. If using both sugar and lemon, pour the tea into the cup, put the sugar in the tea, and then add the lemon. If using only lemon, pour in the tea and then add the lemon. Avoid adding both milk and lemon, as the lemon may cause the milk to curdle.

- As you stir your tea, make as little noise as possible.

- Place the saucer in the palm of your non-dominant hand, with the fingers spread slightly. Hold the teacup in your dominant hand with your index finger through the handle, the thumb just above it for support, and your middle finger below the handle. The remaining fingers should curl naturally around the cup. Do not extend your pinkie.

- Pair each food course with a different tea. See suggestions for pairing foods with various teas on pages 118 to 123 ("How to Pair Tea and Food").

Tips for Eating

- Unfold your napkin on your lap below table level. If you must leave your chair briefly for any reason, place the napkin on the chair, not on the table.

- Whether the foods are served on multi-tiered trays or on separate plates, they should be eaten in courses. Eat savories such as finger sandwiches first, followed by scones, and then finish with sweets.

- Most foods can be eaten with your fingers if they are small and easy to handle.

- Add just enough jam, citrus curd, or clotted cream, or all of these toppings, to your plate for your scones. Scones should be cut in half horizontally with a knife. Using your knife or a butter spreader, you can add a small amount of jam, curd, or clotted cream, or a little of all of them, to each half, you can add it as you go for each bite, or you can break off a small piece and add it individually to each piece. Add the jam or curd before the clotted cream.

High Tea

Members of the working class in England enjoyed their tea as well, though they did so in a different fashion. During the Industrial Revolution, workers spent long hours in factories, mines, and similar workplaces that left no time for frivolous entertainment, so they developed their own teatime, which they called "high tea." The name reflected the height of the kitchen or dining room table where the tea was served. Because it was held at the end of a long workday with hungry appetites in mind, this meal was also known as "meat tea." It always included strong tea, and depending on the household, a variety of cheeses, potted pies, cold meats, bacon, bread, and desserts. The menu was just what hardworking people needed when they gathered with their families after a strenuous day's labor.

After a while, high tea was adopted by those outside the working class. Members of the upper class gave their servants Sundays off. Putting together a high tea without the help of their household staff was easy for this wealthy crowd: they simply placed their leftovers on the sideboard. Of course, the types of food served were more luxurious and plentiful than what the lower classes ate.

Today, the term *high tea* is often mistakenly used to describe a more sophisticated or elaborate version of afternoon tea. But high tea remains what it was in the past: a suppertime tea that is much less formal than afternoon tea. An easy way to serve an early evening meal, it might include a tray of cheeses and cold meats, with crackers, a hearty bread, jam, and butter on the side; a hot meat dish such as a meat pie or sausages; fruits, one or two desserts; and, of course, tea. It can be served buffet-style or family-style, and an alcoholic beverage is sometimes added to the table.

English Tea Terms

Because tea is arguably the most popular beverage in England, the English have come up with half a dozen teatimes throughout the day. Some of them are not as commonly observed as others, of course, but any one of them would be a nice addition to your own teatime customs.

- Elevenses is a midmorning tea break, much like the American coffee break. A simple snack is served along with the tea.

- Cream tea is tea and scones with clotted cream, lemon curd, or jam.

- Light tea or dessert tea is a cream tea with the addition of desserts.

- Afternoon tea consists of tea, finger sandwiches, scones, and desserts.

- Royal tea is an afternoon tea that includes a glass of Champagne or sherry.

- High tea is a hearty, casual meal of cold cuts, cheeses, a meat pie or sausages, breads, and desserts usually served in the early evening.

MOROCCAN TEA CEREMONY

Long before tea was commonplace in Morocco, locals drank herbal infusions, the most popular of which was a tisane made with the mint (*na'na*) that grew in the country's mountainous regions. Then, in the mid-nineteenth century, the British, who were unable to deliver their cargoes of Chinese green tea to Baltic ports during the Crimean War, decided to open a new Mediterranean market and unloaded their ships at the Moroccan ports of Tangier and Mogador (present-day Agadir). The Moroccans quickly took to the exotic beverage, mixing the green tea with the mint of their favorite tisane, and a national tea-drinking tradition was born.

Jokingly called Berber whiskey, Moroccan-style tea is consumed throughout the day and far into the evening. In the past, a formal tea ceremony was often performed for guests, though that is less common today. Yet the serving of Moroccan tea remains an art form. Although the tea is not difficult to make, you will need some essentials:

- A teapot, or *barrad*, which is usually made of silver plate, aluminum, or stainless steel. It has a rounded body, a domed lid, and a long curved spout that is perfect for pouring from a great height.

- Heat-resistant, colorful Moroccan tea glasses, usually adorned with ornate gilding, rich patterns, or both.

- Chinese Gunpowder tea, fresh spearmint, sugar, and sometimes, depending on the region, lemon verbena, saffron, orange blossoms, or other spices.

- A round silver or brass tray on which to place all of the tea items.

Brewing Moroccan tea is not difficult. But you may need to practice serving the tea a few times before you achieve the desired frothy finish on each glass. Here are the directions for an everyday contemporary Moroccan tea ceremony.

1. Heat water in a kettle. When the water boils, pour some into the teapot to warm it and then pour the water out.

2. Next, add the tea—about 1 teaspoon tea per 6 oz/170 ml hot water—to the warmed teapot.

3. Add boiling water to the pot, quickly rinse the tea leaves by swirling the teapot, and discard the water.

4. Add fresh mint to the teapot, filling the pot about three-fourths full.

5. Add sugar to the pot. Moroccans use 3 to 5 teaspoons sugar for each 6 oz/ 170 ml water.

6. Pour boiling water over the tea and mint, re-cover the pot, and allow the tea to steep for 3 to 5 minutes. Sometimes Moroccans put their teapot directly on the stove and allow the water to come to a boil again.

7. After the tea has steeped, you can pour the tea. This is where the art of the ceremony comes in. The Moroccans like to aerate the tea, which creates a desirable froth on the top. To do this, when pouring the tea, you must hold the pot as high above the glasses as possible. Then, to aerate the tea further, pour the tea back into the pot and once again, holding the

pot high in the air, pour the tea into the glasses. If you like, repeat this back and forth one more time. Pouring the tea in this manner takes practice, and Moroccans consider mastering this step important because it infuses the flavors of the tea, which makes the tea taste better. Once the flavors have infused, serve the tea.

TEATIME, FRENCH STYLE

Tea was first poured in the French court and in the homes of the French aristocracy about the same time Catherine of Braganza was brewing pots in the Palace of Whitehall. Louis XIV reportedly drank it for health reasons—an aid to digestion—though at least one French physician of the time was quick to denounce the practice, declaring tea "the impertinent novelty of the century." That opinion did not seem to bother the Marquise de Sévigné, the famed letter writer of her day who refers to the flourishing custom of *le thé de cinq heures* (a nod to the classic teatime of England) in at least one of her missives.

Although tea drinking in France faded somewhat after its early popularity, it is in vogue once again. The marquise's term has evolved into

Moroccan Sugar Cubes

The classic sugar for making Moroccan tea comes in an extremely hard cone (or sometimes rectangular block) about 8 in/20 cm long. A copper hammer is traditionally used to break off the amount needed for a pot of tea. The sugar cones are readily available in Morocco, where they are often given as gifts at family get-togethers. Because they are difficult to find outside of Morocco, granulated white sugar may be substituted.

le five o'clock, and the French are sitting down in serene, formal *salons de thé* all over the country. They tend to enjoy a wide variety of teas, both blended and single estate, all of them typically steeped in lovely porcelain pots. More than half of all French tea drinkers add sugar to their cup, about a quarter of them add milk or lemon, and nearly a third of them add nothing. More often than not, the tea is accompanied with one of the exquisite pastries—fruit tart, petit four, macaron, financier—for which the country's bakers are known.

RUSSIAN RITUALS

Late in the seventeenth century, Russia and China signed a treaty that defined both trade and territory, and Russia began importing tea from China. Government-controlled caravans of hundreds of camels made their way across desert sands and mountainous terrain to bring tea—and cotton and silk—to St. Petersburg, a journey that took more than a year. Not surprisingly, once the tea was marketed, its price was so high that only the wealthy could afford it.

In 1735, Czarina Elizabeth, whether because she liked tea or she saw a good business opportunity, launched private caravan trade, and the price of tea fell. By the last decade of the eighteenth century, Russians of all classes were reportedly drinking more than 3.5 million pounds/ 1.6 million kilograms of tea a year, both brick and loose leaf. The tea-caravan trade continued to grow until the mid-nineteenth century, when it peaked. Then, around 1900, the earliest leg of the Trans-Siberian Railway was completed, and the days of the tea caravan were numbered. The train carried much more tea at one time and carried it faster than camels could. That meant that more tea was available more quickly and at lower prices. Tea has been a mainstay of Russian life ever since, driven by the national philosophy that "teatime is all the time."

Although the Russians do not conduct a formal tea ceremony, they did invent a unique piece of tea-making equipment: the samovar. It is basically a hot-water heater—a cross between an urn and a kettle, with a spigot near the base, a chimney for draft, and a ring on top on which to set a small teapot. Both the base and the teapot are made of metal. Some have theorized that it was an adaptation of the Mongolian firepot. Research indicates that the first samovar factory was likely opened in the city of Tula in the late 1770s. Older versions of the samovar were either coal or charcoal fired; newer ones are powered with electricity.

To make tea using a samovar, the samovar is filled with water, which is then brought to a boil. Next, a little of the hot water is swirled around in the teapot to heat it and then discarded. Then, a heaping scoop of loose tea (the exact measurement is up to the tea maker) and some water are added to the teapot and the tea is left to steep for an indefinite amount of time to make a strong tea concentrate, known as the *zavarka*. To serve the tea, each teacup is filled with a small amount of tea concentrate and then topped off with boiling water from the spigot. The ratio of tea to water depends on how strong a brew is desired. Finally, the teapot with the remaining concentrate is placed on top of the samovar to keep it warm until the next cup of tea is served. It is easy to see how this ingenious contraption allows Russians to keep a pot of tea going all day long.

Russians traditionally serve tea in clear glass cups—tea glasses, really—with silver holders decorated with engraved pictures and enamel inlays. Black tea is the most commonly drunk tea. Tea is always served hot, and as soon as a child is old enough to sit at the table, he or she is old enough to drink tea with the family. It is said by Russians that "tea completes the deal," meaning that tea is used to finish a meal. It also puts a different accent on a snack, turning it into a mini meal that allows you sit down and relax for a bit.

When anyone stops by for a visit at a Russian home, he or she is shown a place to sit and invited to have tea. This is an age-old custom and failing to extend the courtesy is considered the height of rudeness. Also, the phrase "having tea" never means just drinking the infusion. Rather, it is tea along with everything from a small snack to a dessert to a full meal. The service is defined by what you have on hand in your kitchen and how much time you and your guests have to spend together.

Russians typically add lemon and sugar or sometimes honey to their tea. In the nineteenth century, a cup of tea was commonly sweetened by the drinker holding a sugar cube in his or her mouth as the tea was sipped, and some traditionalists still enjoy drinking their tea this way. Flavored teas are seldom imbibed in Russia, but some tea drinkers enjoy spooning a few mashed raspberries or black currants into their teacup. Tea is also sometimes served with a little saucer of *varenye*, a loose, sweet dark cherry preserve. The tea drinker spoons some of the *varenye* into his or her mouth and follows it with a sip of tea.

Tea Etiquette, Iranian Style

The Iranians share a connection with the Russian tea tradition through the samovar. Most likely introduced to Iran by Russian traders more than two centuries ago, this iconic Russian "appliance" is ubiquitous in Iranian households. And also as in Russia, tea is drunk throughout the day and evening, and no visitor enters a house without being offered a cup.

As I began to study the tea-drinking traditions of Iran, I came across an interesting example of Iranian etiquette known as *tarof*. My Iranian friends have confirmed this practice, and although most of them think it is outdated, others insist that to be recognized as having good manners, one must observe it. *Tarof* is a way of showing modesty, dignity, and restraint in a back-and-forth gesture between two parties. It is demonstrated by always refusing to eat something when first asked.

When offered tea in Iran, you are invariably offered some kind of treat, called *shirini*, as well. To show good manners, you must refuse the treat politely even if you desire it and are hungry. The host must then be more insistent in offering it to you, and you must more emphatically but politely turn it down. By the third time, the host will practically put the treat on a plate and hand the plate to you. Only then may you accept the offer and enjoy the snack with your tea.

TEA AND MEDITATION

Tea has been used as a part of meditation from its earliest days as a drink. Indeed, tea and meditation are a natural fit. As detailed in "What Is In Your Tea?" (page 139), the beverage contains many natural properties that help the body relax, slow down, unwind, let go. That makes it the perfect beverage to sip when you want your mind and body to go into a contemplative state. Donna Fellman, author of *Tea Here Now*, says, "It is an incredible act of courage to tell yourself you need balance and to allow yourself to feel the stillness with your infusion in your hands."

Other tea ceremonies and rituals are typically about time spent with others and the proper way to conduct the procedure. For the meditation tea ritual, you are alone and relaxed, and the methodology of making tea is not the focus. Zen master and author Thich Nhat Hanh has described this marriage between tea and meditation particularly eloquently: "When I drink tea, there is only me and the tea. The rest of the world dissolves. There are no worries about the future. No dwelling on past mistakes . . . I drink the tea, the essence of the leaves becoming a part of me. I am informed by the tea, changed. This is the act of life, in one pure moment, and in this act the truth of the world suddenly becomes revealed. All the complexity, pain, drama of life is a pretense, invented in our minds for no good purpose. There is only the tea, and me, converging."

So what is tea meditation? The great news is that it can be what you want it to be. You will, however, need a place where you feel at peace just being in it. For those who can afford the luxury, it can mean a separate building that is your private teahouse. For others, it can mean a room in your house or elsewhere that is used solely for this purpose. For still others, it can be a chair or a mat in a room that is also used for other activities.

My home office, which I also call my tearoom, is where I like to sit quietly with my tea. It is the sunroom of our home and has windows on three sides. I can close myself off with French doors from the rest of the house and the world. Outside the sunroom, I can see lush trees and woods that look new with the arrival of each season. This is my space, and even though I work in it, I can find stillness there. I cannot work, I cannot be creative, in a place that isn't beautiful. The space is uncluttered and carefully filled with special things that I love, such as teapots, tea books, pictures of my family, and pillows inscribed with Darjeeling, Ceylon, Provence, and other evocative names. I drink tea all day long there as I work at my desk, but when I need to escape, I move to my leather chair in the corner of the room that faces out to the woods. That is where I sit with my cup of tea and meditate.

If the weather is nice, sometimes I step through the sunroom door that opens onto a small outdoor patio. There, I sit in my Adirondack rocker with my teacup in hand and allow myself to be with God's beauty.

Some practitioners incorporate the preparation of the beverage into the ritual; for others the ritual begins once the tea is ready. Donna Fellman's tearoom has a chaise lounge in it as well as a tea kettle, tea, and other necessary equipment, so that making the tea is part of her meditation. I don't include the preparation of the tea as part of my ritual. I wait for my infusion to be ready, and then I go to my chair, close the doors, and allow myself just to be. My form of meditation is rather informal. I usually start off with a prayer of thanks to God for my tea and the beauty that surrounds me. Then I just breathe, look out at the trees, and allow my mind to be in the moment. Thoughts come and go, but I don't allow myself to get caught up in them. When I take the time to meditate, I find that I am much more creative and productive and much less stressed. My writing is better, I am a better wife and mother, and I tend to have a better outlook on life.

The beauty of this ritual is that all you need to begin is a small, still space and some basic brewing equipment, tea, and water. You owe it to yourself to take the time to experience the stillness.

CHAPTER FOUR

BEYOND THE CUP

Pairing, Cooking, Cocktails, and More

Tea can be "consumed" in a number of ways beyond simply brewing and sipping. You can cook with it, mix it into cocktails, use it to soothe a sunburn or bring down the welt from a bug bite, work its spent leaves into a compost pile, or even dye a shirt with it. But before I explain how to create tea-infused vodka for a round of martinis or make a tea-based paste to fight a mosquito bite, I will introduce you to one of the most interesting activities involving tea, which is pairing it with food. When done correctly, it reveals nuances in the tea that go undetected when it is drunk on its own. The first step in understanding how to pair food and tea is to meet the tea sommelier.

THE TEA SOMMELIER

Move over, wine sommeliers. There's a new kid on the block: the tea sommelier. According to *Webster's Collegiate Dictionary*, the word *sommelier* derives from the Middle French *soumelier*, or an "official charged with transportation of supplies," which probably in turn derives from an Old French word for "pack animal driver." It was not until the nineteenth century that *sommelier* came to mean a "wine steward," which is why the tea industry feels comfortable adopting the term.

But can the duties of a wine sommelier be equated with those of a tea sommelier? Wine sommeliers are expertly trained professionals who work in high-end restaurants and hotels where they source wines and create wine lists, oversee the storage of wines, train employees about the inventory, and have a sophisticated knowledge of the origin and flavor profile of individual wines. They also talk about the wines with the guests, first exploring a guest's taste preferences and then trying to suggest a wine that both satisfies those preferences and pairs well with the food that has been chosen. Finally, many of them travel around the globe to vineyards and food and wine conferences to keep up with what's new in the wine world.

Specialty teas are becoming just as highly regarded as fine wines in some establishments, and that means that tea sommeliers are being hired to do the same things for tea—source and develop lists, oversee inventory, train the staff, guide the guests, and travel the world—as their wine counterparts do for wine. And serious tea drinkers are reaping the rewards.

In the Western world, the first acting tea sommelier on the scene was Helen Gustafson, although the title was never bestowed her. A tea drinker since her childhood, Gustafson was enamored with tea and tea parties. In the early 1970s, she was hired as a hostess at the newly opened and now famed Chez Panisse restaurant in Berkeley, California, where the kitchen has used local, seasonal, sustainably raised ingredients since its early days. Unhappy with the quality of tea being served in a restaurant known for its superior fresh foods, Gustafson soon began to source and buy the best specialty teas and train the staff on their correct preparation. She also bought and cared for all of the tea accessories and taught weekly classes on tea at Chez Panisse for patrons and staff alike. She stayed at the restaurant for twenty years, and although she did not have the formal title of tea sommelier—no one did at the time—many in the industry credit her with leading the charge that has resulted in fine-dining establishments improving their tea service.

James Labe was another early tea sommelier and the first official one to carry the title. In 1997, chef Michel Nischan opened the Heartbeat restaurant in the W Hotel in Manhattan and hired Labe to oversee the tea service. Some say Nischan was ahead of his time in treating the tea menu with the same respect as the wine menu. But Nischan, who is now an award-winning cookbook author and chef-owner of the Dressing Room in Westport, Connecticut, opened with the late Paul Newman, sees it differently: "When we created Heartbeat restaurant, we based the concept on the guests' well-being and focused on local, organic, sustainable foods … I realized that our concept might attract vegetarians, vegans, and other enlightened diners, some of whom might not wish to drink wine or any other alcoholic beverage with their meal. I already had an appreciation for the artisanship behind truly great teas, so I decided we needed a tea list. We found James working at the cheese counter at Balducci's, and although he was a cheese expert, all he really wanted to talk about was tea. It was at that moment that I knew we had 'our man.' We hired James to source, select, and individually brew all of our teas, and to go from table to table with a list of teas and explain the virtues and origin of each one—much like a great sommelier does for wine. We soon dubbed James our tea sommelier—the first ever in the country! An explosion of interest from *Saveur*, *Gourmet*, and other national and international press followed. It created quite the buzz!"

Because the world of specialty tea was so new in the United States, Labe spent a lot of his time educating both the staff and the clientele. He also helped pair tea with the food on the menu to ensure a well-rounded culinary journey for the guests and organized special dining events that paired a different tea with each course.

Since then, the position of tea sommelier has expanded around the globe, and its popularity continues to grow slowly. The Tea Association of Canada started a certified tea sommelier program at George Brown College in Toronto, Ontario, that is now offered through approved colleges throughout the country. The first group of certified tea sommeliers graduated in 2009 by completing all eight courses offered in the curriculum and passing an examination. Jim Nicholson, an early graduate of the program, summed up the curriculum and his role as a tea sommelier this way: "At George Brown College, I took courses on the historical roots of tea, the geographical varieties of tea, the cultural practices and connections to tea, proper preparation and tea tasting, sensory development, tea garden and food industry management, and food pairing. This is the academic side of becoming a tea sommelier. I have met many tea masters and experts who know more about tea than I will ever know. The difference is the tea sommelier is trained in the macro-view of tea as a product, an industry, and an art form, but most of all as a pleasure!"

London Tea Sommelier Karl Kassab Sets the Record Straight

Some people might think that being a tea sommelier is a glamorous job that allows you to sit around all day and sip tea and talk with people about the brew. This is far from the truth. Although a lot of tea tasting may be going on in a day, it is typically professional tasting, or cupping (see page 79, "Professional Cupping"), rather than casual sipping. Plus, the job does not stop at tasting tea.

In 2011, I had the pleasure of interviewing Karl Kassab, London's first tea sommelier, who is quick to point out the irony of a man from Algiers becoming the first British tea sommelier. I met him at Apsleys restaurant in the Lanesborough Hotel, where he began working in 1995 and was integral in introducing a sophisticated tea service and where he remained until recently.

Kassab has been around tea since he was a child in Algeria. But it was not until after he moved to London and took classes offered through the United Kingdom Tea Council, studied alongside tea brokers, and pursued research on his own that he was able to achieve the title of tea sommelier in 2003. What were his duties as a tea sommelier? They evolved over the years. In the beginning, he primarily guided patrons through the restaurant's tea list and trained his staff to do the same. But as time passed, his duties increased. He worked an average of twelve to fourteen hours a day, starting early in the morning with breakfast service at the hotel. He was in charge of sourcing teas from wholesalers, brokers, and sometimes directly from a tea garden or estate, all of which is time-consuming because each year's crop is different. After receiving samples of the teas in which he was interested, he spent a lot of time cupping them to determine what he wanted on the menu. He was responsible for developing new blends to offer customers as well, so that the hotel would continue to be a trendsetter.

He consulted directly with the head pastry chef, who developed tea-infused pastries for the hotel's award-winning afternoon tea service. When afternoon rolled around, he was on duty in the restaurant explaining to customers the extensive list of teas. He helped them select teas to pair with the seasonally changing sweet and savory selections on the menu, encouraging them to try a different infusion with each course that matches both the food and the customers' personal preferences. And because he couldn't be everywhere at once, he took time to train the restaurant staff in how to suggest seasonally sensitive pairings of tea and food.

As you can see, a tea sommelier is more about long hours and hard, detailed work than it is about glamour. And after enjoying afternoon tea with Karl Kassab and his staff, I can attest that the several United Kingdom Tea Council awards bestowed on the Lanesborough for serving the best afternoon tea in the city are well deserved.

The curriculum of the Tea Sommelier Academy in Colombo, Sri Lanka, includes learning about tea not only in a classroom but also in the tea fields, where students follow the production of tea from its plucking to its packaging. They also attend the Colombo tea auction where buyers from around the planet come to purchase Ceylon teas.

In Germany, there are currently two training programs for people who want to excel in tea service. One of them, which began in 2007 and is cosponsored by the German Chamber of Commerce and a private tea company, includes four blocks of classroom training consisting of three to four days each, with testing after each block, and an apprenticeship during which students learn how to work directly with customers. The final examination has two parts: the students first discuss teas orally and then brew various types of infusions. The second German program, which dates to 2003 and is operated by a private tea company, includes classroom study, practical training through tastings and different preparation methods, and then hands-on training in different growing regions of Sri Lanka.

Additional tea sommelier programs have been started in Argentina, the Netherlands, and France, among other countries. As of this writing, the United States does not yet have a high-quality formal training program. However, a group of tea professionals who have taught classes in tea and food pairing and who have worked in the hospitality industry as tea sommeliers are seeking to create an American program that would involve standards for testing.

HOW TO PAIR TEA AND FOOD

One of the areas of study for any tea sommelier is the art of pairing tea and food. Every pairing should expose new aspects of both the tea and the food that neither one could achieve if consumed on its own. Although accomplishing that may sound difficult, it actually is not, once you have grasped a handful of basic pairing principles.

I enjoy teaching classes on tea and food pairing to both industry people and the general public. For many attendees outside the industry, my class is the first time they are exposed to the idea that tea can pair wonderfully with food. It is fascinating for me to see the looks on their faces as they sample the chosen pairing and discover a new culinary delight. That response is what most instructors hope to see when students uncover something new and interesting for the first time. As you begin to put together your first pairings, I hope that you will experience that same delight.

I appreciate combinations of tea and food based on simplicity. I am originally from the Pays Basque region of southwestern France, near Spain. A lot of sheep's milk cheeses are produced in the Pyrenees Mountains that border the area, and one of my favorites is Ossau-Iraty. It can be described as having a Gruyère-like sweetness that builds to nutty and then tops off with a hit of sharp acidity, before cascading down to an earthy and light grassiness. The cheese matches perfectly Butterfly of Taiwan, a mellow oolong with wood and honey notes that linger in the mouth.

FRANÇOIS-XAVIER DELMAS
FOUNDER, LE PALAIS DES THÉS

Pairing tea and food is much like pairing wine and food, with one beverage traded out for the other, so if you are knowledgeable about the latter, you are well on your way to doing the same with tea. First, you must fully understand what defines each of the six classes of tea described in chapter one. The next step is to learn how to steep and then taste teas to identify their flavor profiles and their nuances, which I covered in chapter two. Now, you are ready to begin pairing.

A good pairing really comes down to what feels right in your mouth—in other words, a pairing must have good mouthfeel. One aspect to consider is the weight of the food compared to that of the tea. For example, if you are trying to pair a steak with a tea, you will need to choose a bold tea that can stand up to the robustness of the meat, like an Indian black Assam or Sri Lankan black Ceylon, to name just two possibilities. Or let's say you want to pair a lighter food, like sea scallops, with a tea. In this case, you want to choose a light tea that will not overwhelm the delicateness of the seafood, such as a Chinese green Dragon Well. If there is a sauce involved with the steak or the scallops, you will need to consider its weight as well when choosing a tea.

The level of fat in a dish also affects your tea choice. When you eat dishes that are high in fat, your mouth becomes coated with it, producing a distinctive mouthfeel. As an example, think about how your mouth feels after you eat a high-quality milk chocolate truffle or a piece of creamy Brie. An astringent tea, a type found in a number of classes, will cut through the fattiness of the food, quickly transforming your mouth into a welcome resting place. An Indian black first flush Darjeeling, which is not only astringent because of its high tannin levels but also wonderfully floral and sweet, with a slight muscatel-like fruitiness, would be a good choice. By clearing the palate between bites, each bite is fully tasted.

All of this talk about the importance of mouthfeel when choosing teas has been verified by science. A study published in October 2012 by Paul Breslin of Rutgers University and the Monell Chemical Senses Center points out that "the mouth is a magnificently sensitive organ, arguably the most sensitive in the body. The way foods make our mouths feel has a great deal to do with what foods we choose to eat. If you notice how we eat fatty foods in general, we tend to pair them with something astringent. They go together because they balance each other out. The opposition between fatty and astringent sensations allows us to eat fatty foods more easily if we also ingest astringents with them."

Another factor to consider when pairing is whether you want the food and the tea to complement, contrast, or balance each other. Here, you need to think about weight and fat level plus the elements of flavor: sweet, sour, salty, bitter, and umami. If you want the tea and food to complement each other, choose a tea that will match or mirror the flavor components in the dish. If the dish is sweet, for example, choose a naturally sweeter tea, such as a Chinese black Lychee. A spicy dish often prompts a pairing based on contrast. For example, a spice-laden hot curry would pair well with a sweet oolong with a long finish, such as Taiwanese Oriental Beauty, which will cut through the burning sensation in your mouth. Or you might decide to contrast a salty dish such as country ham with a sweet tea, like a Chinese black Golden Yunnan, or a salty cheese such as French Comté with a naturally sweet Japanese green high-quality Sencha. Alternatively, you could pair it with an herbal choice, such as a Korean hydrangea leaf tisane (from *Hydrangea serrata*, a species native to the Korean Peninsula and Japan), which naturally brews up sweet, as if sugar had been added. A balanced pairing is one in which the tea and the food not only complement each other but also become a harmonious couple with neither one dominant. Sipping a Chinese Golden Monkey tea with its chocolaty notes while eating a piece of semisweet chocolate is a good example.

The final aspect to consider with tea and food pairing is the origin of both. Some chefs and wine sommeliers believe that "if it grows together, it goes together." As an example, reflect on how well a Chianti wine goes with pasta dressed with a tomato sauce. To a certain degree, this approach works with teas as well. For example, Japanese food pairs exceptionally well with Japanese teas. But because tea cultivation is restricted to relatively few countries, this pairing approach cannot be widely applied.

My favorite pairings are not from elaborate menus. What gives me the most pleasure is a simple pairing like Pu'erh with ripe strawberries, or a delicate Keemun with honeydew melon. The tea and fruit each open up the palate to the flavors of the other, accentuating everything.

JAMES LABE
AMERICA'S FIRST TEA SOMMELIER

People often ask me for a list of pairings of particular foods with particular teas so that they can follow them exactly. I never supply the list for two reasons. First, there are no definitive pairings of tea and food. Pairing them is an art and a science—and a pleasurable journey that each tea drinker should take. Second, every individual's palate is different, and what may be a highly pleasing pairing to one person may not be as wildly appealing to another. For example, when I give seminars on tea and food pairing, I always try to offer two different teas with each food to demonstrate that no single correct pairing exists. Invariably when I ask the class to raise their hands to indicate which tea paired best, the room is split just about down the middle. In the end, it is what you think is good that really matters. Or, as eighth-century Chinese scholar Lu Yu observed in his definitive work, *The Classic of Tea,* "In the end, goodness is for the mouth to decide."

Despite my just saying that I don't like to supply a list of pairings, I am putting one here to get your creative juices flowing. These have been some of my favorite pairings over the years, and I am including these ideas only because I hope they will inspire you to get started on your own list.

- Toast with a sweet lavender raspberry jam and a slightly smoky Chinese black Keemun

- Scone with a tangy lemon curd and an astringent black Indian first flush Darjeeling

- Carrot cake with a Chinese black Golden Yunnan

- White chocolate with a nutty Chinese green Dragon Well

- Bittersweet chocolate with an earthy Chinese Pu'erh

- Mushrooms with an earthy Chinese Pu'erh

- Roast turkey or duck with a toasty Chinese Tie Guanyin oolong

- Roast lamb with a sweet, mildly astringent Chinese black Keemun

- Grilled steak with a malty Indian black Assam

- Grilled nonoily fish with a sweet vegetal green Japanese Sencha

- Lobster or scallops with a floral, lightly oxidized Taiwanese Jade oolong

- Spicy curries with a bold, lightly sweetened Sri Lankan black Ceylon with milk
- Texas-style barbecue with a lightly sweetened brisk iced tea or a lightly sweetened peach-flavored iced tea

---

When it comes to tea and food pairing, without a doubt, my favorite pairings are tea and cheese. I love these pairings for a couple of reasons. First, they can be rapturous! All aspects of tea—tannin levels, mouthfeel, flavor, intensity, aromatics, temperature—can come into play. Most important, however, I like the fact that these pairings tend to take people by surprise. People don't usually think about tea and cheese together, and guiding them through these pairings can help to point out the parallels between fine teas and fine wines. I want people to begin to look at tea with the respect, desire, and expectations that they so often reserve for wine.

CYNTHIA GOLD
TEA SOMMELIER AND CHEF

COOKING WITH TEA

Using tea in recipes isn't a new concept. It was used as an ingredient in China soon after its discovery there, and it has been used in cooking elsewhere in Asia for centuries. The Tibetans, for example, combine tea from a Pu'erh brick, water, and salt, bring the mixture to a boil, strain it, add yak butter, and churn everything together, much like churning butter, to make what they call butter tea. They both drink the tea and add it to roasted barley flour, known as *tsampa*, to make a dish with a doughlike consistency called *paak*. The Burmese use pickled tea leaves, known as *lahpet*, in a popular saladlike dish, and Japanese cooks have long made broths and rice dishes with tea.

Today, many chefs are experimenting with new ways to incorporate tea in their cooking, and you can, too. As you work with tea in your kitchen, keep in mind that you want it to be the "secret ingredient" in the recipe that folks will taste but will still wonder what it is. In other words, no dish should scream out that it has tea in it. The best dishes are always a blend of ingredients, with each ingredient complementing, rather than overpowering, the others.

There is something quite magical that happens when I have the chance to cook with tea. My end goal is never to make something taste like one particular tea, but instead to meld the flavors together just as a violin is a part of an orchestra. One recipe that comes to mind is a winter vegetable soup I made with homemade udon noodles and a Pu'erh broth. I infused the Pu'erh tea with dehydrated royal trumpet mushrooms and then simmered it with various spices. The end result was a very rich and earthy broth with spicy notes. I added some finely ground Hojicha (roasted Japanese green tea) to the udon dough to impart a slightly roasted flavor to the noodles. I served the broth with roasted kabocha squash, sweet baby turnips, kale, and wild mushrooms. Eating the dish gave me the same calm, grounded feeling that I have when I drink Pu'erh. At the same time, it conjured up memories of my beloved winters in New York.

MELANIE FRANKS
CHEF AND CERTIFIED TEA SPECIALIST

Consider how various teas taste before you begin adding them to food. Tea flavors run the gamut from floral, earthy, grassy, astringent, clean, and brisk to deep and hearty. You might start by adding tea to recipes you already make, so that you can easily detect its presence, before trying your new secret ingredient in an original creation. Finally, just as when you use wine in cooking, don't use a tea that you would not drink. You don't need to use the highest-priced teas in your kitchen, but they should be of good quality. Here are some ideas to get you started on incorporating tea in your cooking.

Tea Steeped in Water

I like to add flavor to dishes by using tea as a substitute for the usual liquid or by combining it with the usual liquid. This is great for soups, stews, braises, and marinades; for steaming; and for cooking grains such as rice. If you want a concentrated flavor, make a concentrate: Add three to six times the amount of tea that you would customarily add to the steeping water, then steep the tea for the usual amount of time. Some folks think that if they steep the tea longer than usual, they will get a better concentrate. The contrary is true, what you will get is oversteeped tea that can be quite bitter.

One of my favorite ways to use a tea concentrate is for poaching chicken for chicken salad.

It gives the meat a haunting flavor that will liven up even the most basic salad. I also like to add a concentrate to a barbecue sauce. Chinese black Lapsang Souchong has a wonderful smoky flavor that ensures your barbecue sauce will have a great smoky bite without having to add liquid smoke. A concentrate is also good for thinning a sauce or soup or for deglazing a roasting pan before making gravy. Try using it for making a sorbet or a simple syrup, too.

Sweet iced tea is known as the table wine of the American South, and Southern cooks have found that adding a sweetened tea concentrate to their meat and poultry brines does wonders, especially for chicken. The brined chicken is then tossed on the grill or, you guessed it, fried. The tea-treated brine will give the chicken a nuanced flavor that will keep guests guessing what the ingredient is.

Tea Steeped in Other Liquids

You can steep tea in liquids other than water with good results. The steeping time will vary with the liquid because different liquids have different solubility rates. That means that you will have to experiment and keep tasting until you get the taste you like. A good way to add tea to desserts is to steep it in the cream you use to make truffles or in the custard for home-made ice cream. You can use this same method

for cream soups. The high fat in the cream adheres to the essential oils naturally present in tea, which produces a superb result.

Some other liquids to consider are vinegars, fruit juices, and even spirits, which I discuss more fully in the section on tea cocktails on page 128. You can use a cold-steep method when adding the leaves to fruit juices and spirits, the same method I use for making iced tea (see page 67). For vinegars, you can use the cold-steep or hot-steep method.

Tea Added Directly to a Recipe

Sometimes you can put tea leaves directly into a savory or sweet dish. When I have done this, I grind the leaves first, either with a mortar and pestle or a spice grinder. Do not use a coffee grinder unless it has never been used for coffee. The strong essential oils in coffee beans leave a residue in the grinder that will overwhelm the taste and aroma of tea. You can also use Matcha or a food-grade green tea powder.

Ground tea leaves are a wonderful addition to rubs for meats and other proteins before grilling or baking. They can also be added to the dough for a pie, quiche, or tart crust or used in cookie, shortbread, or scone dough. You can put them in a frosting or in the topping for a crumble, coffee cake, or muffins. I have also incorporated

ground tea leaves when I make brittle or cara-melized nuts. You can even combine them with salt and sprinkle the mixture over your favorite vegetables.

Smoking with Tea

Smoking indoors can be a little tricky—an exhaust fan is necessary—but it can be done. The first time I tried foods smoked with tea was at a now-closed tearoom in Asheville, North Carolina, that was owned by my friend Tami Halliman. Her chef was quite inventive in the ways he used tea in his recipes, and smoking with tea was just one of them. The tearoom even hosted a seminar at a trade event that I attended on how to smoke with tea, and I learned a number of valuable tips that day.

The best way to smoke with tea is to combine it with raw rice to help maintain the heat. Combine the tea and rice with sugar and other aromatics, such as spices and citrus peels, to create a fragrant smoke, and put the mixture in a wok or in a large, heavy roasting pan that will fit over two burners on your stove top. If you are using a roasting pan, arrange the mixture in two piles so that each pile will be directly over a burner. Place a perforated pan on top of the tea mixture, and then place the items you are smoking on the perforated pan. Put the wok or roasting pan on the stove top and turn on the heat to high. As

soon as the tea mixture begins to smoke, seal the wok or roasting pan tightly with aluminum foil, place a sheet pan or a tight-fitting lid on top to secure the seal, and then turn down the heat to low. The smoke will last fifteen to twenty minutes before the tea mixture begins to burn. At the first sign that the smoke is finished, turn off the heat and allow the setup to stand for another fifteen minutes or so to allow the smoke to permeate the food.

Depending on what you are cooking, the food may need to cook longer. If so, carefully lift off the lid, remove the food and perforated pan from the wok or roasting pan, and discard the spent rice and tea mixture. If you want the food to have a smokier flavor, replace the rice and tea mixture with a new batch and repeat the smoking steps. Or you can finish cooking the food on the stove top or in the oven without additional smoke. Make sure you follow these directions carefully, or your house will fill with smoke.

If smoking indoors sounds too risky, move outdoors to a smoker or grill. To use tea leaves in a smoker, moisten the leaves and follow the smoker manufacturer's instructions for using wood chips. You can smoke with tea alone or mix it with aromatics, wood chips, or both, depending on the flavor you are trying to infuse. If you are using a charcoal or gas grill that has a smoker box, put the moistened tea leaves or tea leaf mixture in the box. If the grill doesn't have a smoker box, enclose the moistened leaves or leaf mixture in a tightly sealed packet fashioned from heavy-duty aluminum foil and poke a few small holes in the top of the packet. Prepare a fire in the grill and place the packet on the grill rack. When smoke starts rising from the smoker box or packet, put the food on the grill, cover the grill so that all of the pungent smoke permeates your food, and grill the food for as long as you would normally grill it. If you are using a charcoal grill, you can skip the smoker box or foil packet and instead place moistened tea leaves directly on the coals once they are covered with white ash, cover the grill, and cook until the food is done.

TEA COCKTAILS: OLD BECOMES NEW AGAIN

Before the now-ubiquitous "cocktail," there was "punch." The origin of punch is a bit sketchy, but most authorities agree that a proper punch included alcohol. According to one of the most-repeated theories on the origin of punch, British sailors brought it back from India in the early seventeenth century. Its name comes from the Hindi word *panch*, or "five," which referred to the five elements used to create a proper balance of five flavors: sweet, sour, weak, alcoholic, and bitter. The corresponding ingredients were, in order, sugar, lemon, water, arrack (a distilled beverage made from the sap of the unopened flowers of the coconut palm), and, not surprisingly given where it was created, tea.

British and American cookbooks from the eighteenth and nineteenth centuries include punch recipes that also call for tea and some sort of alcoholic beverage. Among the oldest of these recipes is English regent's punch, a mixture of tea, citrus juices, sugar, brandy, rum, and Champagne. Around the same time, a similar drink, Saint Cecilia punch, began gaining popularity in the United States. Saint Cecilia is the patron saint of music, and the Saint Cecilia Society, founded in the 1760s in Charleston, South Carolina, started the first subscription concert series in the country. The society later sponsored fancy balls and dinners, at which its eponymous punch, a heady mixture of lemon, pineapple, sugar, tea, brandy, peach brandy, and rum, was served. A tea punch also appeared in the 1839 cookbook *The Kentucky Housewife*. It called for tea concentrate, sugar, cream, and claret or Champagne and could be served hot or cold.

As you can see, blending tea and spirits goes back a long way, and although punch bowls have been replaced with stemmed glasses, the appeal of this mixture remains. (I have heard rumblings that punch is making a comeback, so don't give

away that old punch bowl just yet.) Here are some things to think about before you attempt to create a tea cocktail.

- What class of tea do you want to use? You don't need to use a highly priced tea that is especially good on its own, but it must be a good-quality tea that you enjoy drinking.

- What overall flavor profile are you looking for? Do you fancy fruity, savory, or sweet?

- What is the texture of the drink? Will it be creamy, slushy, or strained over ice?

- What type of spirit do you want to use? (I have made some suggestions; see "Adding Brewed Tea to a Cocktail," following.)

- What is the best method for introducing the tea? Will you use brewed tea, a tea-infused alcohol, or a tea-infused simple syrup?

Adding Brewed Tea to a Cocktail

When you mix tea into a cocktail, you want to make sure the alcohol does not mask the tea. One of the simplest ways is to add tea directly to a cocktail is with a tea concentrate, which you make by adding more tea leaves per 6 oz/170 ml of water than you would if brewing tea for sipping. The desirable strength of the concentrate will depend on the class of tea you are using and the spirit or spirits and other ingredients in the cocktail. Remember, you increase the strength of brewed tea by adding more tea, not by allowing the tea to steep longer, which can turn it bitter. This is a good time to experiment with flavored teas, such as bergamot-tinged Earl Grey, which can yield unique combinations.

I call my favorite tea cocktail creation White Rose. It is a combination of White Peony tea, locally sourced honey, rose water, and great gin. I love it because the flavor combination enhances the botanical side of the gin, which is sometimes overlooked. It also lets the white tea show through in a unique way.

CHRIS CASON
TEA SOMMELIER, TAVALON TEA

Infusing Alcohol with Tea

You can steep tea in different kinds of liquor using the same cold-steep method you use for iced tea (see page 67) by simply trading out the water for the liquor. The steeping time will vary, depending on the type of tea and type of liquor you are using, so you will learn what tastes good to you only by trial and error. Vodka, gin, and port are good spirit suggestions for infusing. What tea you use is limited only by your imagination. If you have tasted a tea you like and you have thought it might be good in a cocktail, give it a try!

Infusing Simple Syrup with Tea

Simple syrup is equal parts water and sugar that have been heated together until the sugar dissolves. You can infuse any tea into this liquid while it is still hot and then strain it once it has cooled. Be sure the liquid is not too hot when using delicate teas, such as white, green, or oolong.

Purchasing Tea-Infused Spirits

A number of companies now sell tea-infused spirits. I have tasted several of them, and I think most of them are good. Some of the companies include ideas on their websites for creating cocktails with their tea-infused spirits, which you might want to try.

TEA BEYOND THE KITCHEN AND THE BAR

Beauty product companies are mixing tea in everything from facial cleansers and eye makeup to antiaging creams and shampoo. Spa operators are promoting tea in bath salts, face masks, and body lotions. At home, folks are using tea's natural healing powers to temper aches and pains and to make their garden grow. Here are some easy, useful ways to put tea to work beyond the kitchen and the bar.

For Healing

Tea can help to alleviate some everyday pain, swelling, and other discomfort quickly and easily.

- To stop dental bleeding and pain, bite down on a moistened tea bag. Some dentists are now even recommending this.

- To relieve pain from sunburn, soak a towel in cold tea and place it over the sunburned areas. It will cool the skin and reduce some of the swelling. For a full-body sunburn, take a cool tea bath by placing tea in a paper tea filter or in cheesecloth and allowing it to steep in the bath water as you soak.

- To reduce swelling and pain from bug bites, make a paste of strongly brewed tea and baking soda and rub it over the bite. I have used this remedy a lot on my kids, and it is amazing how quickly it works!

- To clean a wound when no first-aid kit is on hand, rinse it with tea to help disinfect it until you can wash it properly. You can also put some tea in a paper filter and hold it over the wound to help stop the bleeding.

For Your Body and Beauty

Beauty products can be expensive, so these tips are guaranteed to save you money. I have tried all of them and they work!

- Soak tired or smelly feet in cool steeped tea to help relieve swelling and reduce odor.

- Soak cotton balls in cooled tea (any tea will work, but I think green tea is the best) and place them over your closed eyes to help alleviate dark circles or puffiness (or both). You can make these ahead of time so you have them on hand. Put the tea-soaked cotton balls in a resealable freezer bag; seal it closed, forcing out all the air; and store in the freezer. The soothing cotton balls will be ready to use when you wake up with tired-looking eyes.

- Powdered green tea makes a great facial and body scrub. Mix the powdered tea (can be food grade and not ceremonial grade) with water and some granulated white sugar or large kosher salt and use to cleanse and exfoliate.

- To reduce acne, make a mask by mixing together powdered green tea and water to form a paste. Spread the paste on your face and allow it to dry completely, then rinse it off. The tea helps to draw out the bacteria and to dry oily skin.

- Make a refreshing astringent for your face. My favorite tea for this is Japanese Sencha. Brew the tea and allow it to cool. Transfer it to a spray bottle and spray it on your face for a cooling pick-me-up. It will keep in the refrigerator for up to seven days. It is amazing how refreshing this simple spray is.

- For a quick mouthwash, rinse your mouth with steeped tea. Unlike coffee, tea breath is refreshing.

- Soak your body in a green-tea bath by placing the tea in a paper tea filter or in cheesecloth and allowing it to steep in the bath water as you soak. The tea will help with swelling and make you feel refreshed. If you have aches, add some Epsom salts to the bath.

For Your Garden

Kirsten Kristensen, a certified tea specialist and owner of Tea 4 U, suggests these tips for using tea in your garden. Kirsten is the most ecofriendly person I know, and I deeply respect her for all of her efforts to live "green." She practices these tips along with many others at her home and teahouse.

- Spread used tea leaves over rosebushes and other flower bushes in the garden for nutritious green gardening (tea is antibacterial, so the leaves will help prevent certain bugs and act as a good fertilizer).

- Collect used tea leaves for adding to your compost pile.

- Collect leftover brewed tea in a tea spittoon or bucket (she uses a plastic bucket inside a covered bamboo basket) and use it for watering indoor and outdoor plants.

For Your Home

It is amazing how many ways you can use tea in your home beyond enjoying it as a beverage. I have included just a handful here.

- Sprinkle throughly dried used tea leaves over a carpet that smells a bit musty and leave them for at least ten minutes, then vacuum them up. Both your carpet and your vacuum cleaner will smell fresher.

- Sprinkle thoroughly dried used tea leaves over a dog bed and gently rub in the leaves. (If you are worried about discoloring the bed, don't rub the leaves into the bed, as rubbing the leaves may cause them to leave a stain.) Allow them to stay on the bed for as long as you can, then vacuum them up or carry the bed outside and shake them off. This simple treatment will freshen up a stinky dog bed.

- Sprinkle thoroughly dried used tea leaves into your cat's litter box between cleanings to freshen the scent.

- To help neutralize refrigerator odors, put unused tea leaves (a great use for old tea) in an open container on one of the shelves. The leaves will absorb off odors. This will work for your car or your basement, too.

- Hang a cheesecloth bag of unused tea leaves (another good use for old leaves) in a damp room such as a basement to absorb moisture and lessen musty odors.

- Put thoroughly dried used tea leaves in bowls or glasses with tea candles for a spa-like decoration. The fragrance of the tea blends nicely with the scent of the candle.

- Fill a pillowcase with thoroughly dried used tea leaves to use as your special tea pillow. It may take some time to collect the leaves, but your perseverance will be rewarded. The fragrance from the tea leaves will give you a refreshing and invigorating sleep that is said to enhance memory. (I saw tea pillows in Taiwan and wanted to bring one home, but it was too large to pack.)

- Make sachets of tea leaves and lavender blossoms and place in your dresser drawers to scent your clothes naturally. This sachet is especially good for a lingerie drawer.

- Use a tea concentrate made from black or green tea to dye fabrics.

- Dip a cloth or paper towel into brewed black tea, wring it out, and rub it on paper to "antique" the paper.

Creative Uses for Empty Tea Tins

- Use the tins as decorative candleholders.

- Use the tins as small, cute planters. Before filling a tin, use a nail to make a hole in the bottom for drainage.

- Screw the tins to a cork board or wall and use to organize office supplies.

CHAPTER FIVE

THE BUZZ ABOUT TEA

Caffeine, Health, Coffee, and Sustainability

Do you want to know which tea is the best to drink for good health? Are you confused about tea and caffeine? Are you an avid coffee drinker who is trying to switch to tea? Is consuming only organic and sustainably farmed crops important to you? If you said yes to any of these questions, this chapter is for you.

WHAT IS IN YOUR TEA?

When people ask me what it is I do and I tell them that I am a tea specialist, they typically get a puzzled look on their faces and then ask me what that means. I usually respond by mimicking holding a teacup and putting it up to my mouth to drink. I then say, "Tea, as in the beverage," and an enlightened look comes over their faces. The conversation typically proceeds to them saying that they have never met a tea specialist before and then telling me about their own tea drinking. Invariably, they also say something like, "I try to drink green tea because it is supposed to be good for me, right?"

The answer to that question is not simple. The Chinese drank tea for medicinal purposes long before they drank it for pleasure. But they assumed it was good medicine because of how it made them feel, rather than any scientific proof. Studying the true science behind tea dates only to 1964, and it was not until 1991 that the Tea Council of the USA organized its first global Tea and Human Health Symposium, at which scientists came together to present their research findings to industry professionals and the press. Since then, solid scientific research on this popular worldwide beverage has continued to go forward.

Yet many misconceptions about tea and health continue to plague the media. I am going to go "a little scientific" now, because I think it is important for everyone to understand the language surrounding this topic before trying to answer the question about what tea to drink for good health. Many words, such as *antioxidant*, *free radical*, and *polyphenol*, are regularly used, with the assumption that whoever is listening or reading them understands them. If you don't know what they mean, you are not alone. I have found that when I teach classes about the potentially healthful attributes of tea, most of my students do not know what these terms mean before I fully explain them. What they do know is that antioxidants are good for the body and they should be consuming lots of them, but beyond that, most of the words sound like mumbo jumbo.

The first step to demystifying the language is to understand what is going on inside the *C. sinensis* leaf itself, which will also clear up the confusion on caffeine. Once the basic botanical and chemical makeup of the leaf is understood, the answer to the burning question of which tea is the most healthful will become clearer.

C. sinensis leaves are similar to other plant leaves in their exterior structure and their interior cells. But what makes them different, and what has long intrigued scientists, is that the cells hold some very powerful compounds that can be beneficial to the human body. Understanding a little more about these cells will help you understand why the beverage made from these leaves is good for you. Tea leaves contain proteins, fluoride, and vitamins A, B, C, D, and E. But what especially fascinates researchers are the compounds, the polyphenols, amino acids, and methylxanthines also found in the leaves.

Before we dig more deeply into what these compounds mean for your health, it is important to know that many factors, including the cultivar, growing location, season of the year, light availability, and altitude, determine how much of each of these compounds a tea leaf contains. The age of the leaf is also important. New leaves at the top of the stem have a much different makeup than older leaves farther down on the stem. Typically, a mixture of old and new leaves are plucked to make tea, with the specific number of leaves defined by the class of tea being made and the end quality desired.

Probably the most popular buzzword currently swirling around the subject of tea and health is antioxidant. Essentially, antioxidants are molecules that can help slow down, prevent, and fight off bad things going on in your body (free radicals) that you have acquired through genetics, pollution, or damaging things that you have done to yourself, such as smoking. Many fruits and vegetables contain antioxidants, as does tea.

The broad class of antioxidants known as polyphenols is a naturally occurring family of compounds found in plants, including *C. sinensis*, which appears to be loaded with them. Flavonoids make up the largest subclass of polyphenols. Each plant species and each individual variety within a species has its own unique profile of polyphenols and flavonoids. Postharvest storage and processing can modify this profile.

Here is where you might start getting confused, but it is important to try to pay attention, because this is where you begin to understand the chemical differences among the six classes of tea, according to their level of oxidation. Remember, you want to know what tea is the most healthful to drink, and understanding these chemical differences will help you do just that.

There are six major subclasses of flavonoids. Two of them are a good source of flavonoids in tea, flavonols and catechins, the latter sometimes called flavanols (note the slight difference in spelling). Most of the research on tea and health has focused on catechins, so I will, too. (They are also found in cocoa and chocolate, which is why some health studies lump these foods in with tea.) One of the most abundant catechins is epigallocatechin gallate, which is understandably typically shortened to EGCG.

As the tea leaves are allowed to oxidize, the leaves change color from green to some degree of brown or to black. This chemical transformation is brought on by the enzyme known as polyphenol oxidase, which turns the colorless catechins of green leaves into more complex black tea flavonoids. The action alters not only the color of the tea but also how it tastes and smells. To some degree, this explains why green tea doesn't taste at all like oolong tea, which in turn doesn't taste like black tea. Oolongs have undergone some oxidation in processing, which is why they are called semioxidized, while blacks are fully oxidized.

The two black tea flavonoids that evolve from catechins are called theaflavins and thearubigins, which work together during oxidation. Theaflavins turn the liquor a reddish golden brown and add substantially to the flavor notes. Thearubigins impart a dark brown to black color to the liquor and also give the infusion its clarity, body, and astringency. The tea master decides when the optimal peak for each flavonoid is met for the desired end product.

Now, to wrap up all of this science into a concise statement: As the leaves change color during oxidation, some simple, single catechin molecules (including EGCG) are converted into a more complex array of two primary types of flavonoids, theaflavins and thearubigins. These flavonoids and their catechin parents

Rate of Oxidation and Flavor

The orthodox production method (see page 22, "Orthodox and Nonorthodox Production") allows for a longer oxidation time because the leaves are whole or at least in large pieces. This increases the theaflavins and thus gives the tea more complex flavor notes. Nonorthodox production, which breaks up the leaves into small particles, calls for a shorter oxidation time. This increases the thearubigins, which result in a darker tea with a lot of body but less complexity.

all belong to the broad class of antioxidant phytochemicals known as polyphenols that research has shown are good for us. Just now, scientists have started to study the very complex thearubigins found in black tea. As their knowledge increases about these particular flavonoids, so, too, will the data on black tea's healthful attributes.

As noted previously, the leaf cells of *C. sinensis* contain compounds beyond polyphenol antioxidants that contribute to good health. Among them are methylxanthines, which I discuss in the following section, and amino acids, which play an important role in regulating metabolism and as building blocks of proteins. *C. sinensis* is the only known natural source of the amino acid L-theanine, which makes up about 60 percent of these amino acids in tea and contributes to its aroma. It reaches the brain through the bloodstream rather quickly after consumption and has psychoactive properties, which means it reduces stress, allowing the mind and body to relax. Studies credit this stress reduction with the amino acid's apparent ability to increase the body's levels of serotonin and dopamine, hormones that contribute to our overall sense of well-being.

THE BUZZ ABOUT CAFFEINE

Methylxanthine compounds in the leaves of plants act as deterrents to insects because they impart a bitter taste. Many humans, in contrast, seek out these bitter compounds, especially the best-known member of the family, caffeine. Most of us know that caffeine helps energize us, with just how much varying according to body size and personal tolerance. It is a stimulant that affects the central nervous system, primarily the brain, and metabolism. Although caffeine is the only methylxanthine in coffee, tea contains two others, theophylline and theobromine, both of which are found in chocolate as well. Even though they are considered stimulants, they are also regarded as muscle relaxants that help somewhat counterbalance the negative effects of caffeine on the body.

For a long time, a number of myths plagued discussions of tea and caffeine because sufficient laboratory testing was not available to analyze the relationship accurately. One of the biggest myths was that if you used a quick water wash (that is, if you steeped tea for 30 seconds, threw out the water, and steeped the same leaves again), you would eliminate 80 percent of the caffeine. A second myth was that oxidized teas are higher in caffeine than either semi-oxidized or green teas.

Both of these myths have now been proven false. In the case of the quick water wash, discarding that first batch of steeping water does eliminate caffeine, but the amount is insignificant. The earliest research on this question was done in 1981 and an additional study was done in 1996. Then, in 2008, a study by Dr. Bruce Branan and Micah Buckel of Asbury University, Kentucky, in conjunction with Bruce Richardson of Elmwood Inn Fine Teas confirmed the earlier findings. Although the studies varied slightly in water temperature, steeping time, class of tea, and so on, all three studies found that an insignificant percentage of caffeine was extracted within the first 30 seconds. The 2008 Asbury University study was small, but it closely mimicked preparation procedures commonly used in home preparation. The researchers varied the water temperature and steeped the tea in 7 oz/220 ml of water for three steepings, each at 3 minutes. Eight teas, each from a different origin, were

Decaffeination

To be considered truly decaffeinated for labeling purposes, tea must contain no more than 0.4 percent of caffeine by dry weight. There is no way to eliminate caffeine from tea entirely. Currently, three methods of decaffeinating tea are used, of which only two are approved by the United States Food and Drug Administration. Because all three use some sort of solvent, some of the polyphenols are lost in the decaffeinating process.

ETHYL ACETATE: Considered a natural method because the compound occurs naturally in fruits, vegetables, and other plants, tea leaves are bathed in water, washed with ethyl acetate to remove the caffeine, and then dried. This process is less expensive and removes more polyphenols than the following method, plus some people detect a slight aftertaste.

SUPERCRITICAL CARBON DIOXIDE (CO_2): Also regarded as a natural method because our bodies produce and expel the gas, the leaves are bathed in water and CO_2 that has been pressurized so that it acts like a liquid but maintains the viscosity of a gas as it is pumped through a sealed chamber filled with tea. The CO_2 seeks out and absorbs the caffeine, then the CO_2 is removed and the caffeine is extracted from it using a charcoal filter or water process or both. This procedure is repeated until the desired amount of caffeine has been eliminated, then the leaves are dried. The method is more expensive and keeps more of the polyphenols intact than the ethyl acetate method, plus it does not leave an aftertaste.

METHYLENE CHLORIDE: Known as dichloromethane in Europe, this method is used to decaffeinate tea and coffee in Europe and Canada but is not allowed in the United States for tea, even though it is legal for coffee. It is similar to the ethyl acetate method, and the polyphenol retention level is thought to fall somewhere between the ethyl acetate and CO_2 methods.

analyzed: two whites, two greens, an oolong, and three blacks. The study found that a 3-minute extraction left somewhere between 46 and 70 percent of the caffeine still in the infusion. These findings suggest that if you steep your tea for a short time, throw out the first infusion, and then steep the same leaves again, you will not eliminate a significant amount of the caffeine. You will, however, remove some of the flavor notes and roughly 30 percent of the healthful polyphenol catechins.

There is no quick answer to how much caffeine is in each of the six classes of tea. That's because, as I explained earlier, many factors determine how much of any compound a tea leaf contains. For more insight and a better understanding of what influences the amount of caffeine in a cup of tea, I consulted Nigel Melican, founder and managing director of Teacraft, a leading tea technology and consultancy company. Melican, who has thirty years of hands-on technical experience in the industry, agrees with the large body of soundly researched data that dispels the myth that the darker (more oxidized) the tea, the higher the caffeine level.

But there are ways to evaluate caffeine concentration accurately. One is the age of the leaves, because the higher up on the stem the leaf is, the more concentrated the caffeine will be. That means that the buds and the new young leaves will have the highest levels, which puts Silver Needle white tea at or near the top of the list. It also discredits the idea that the lightest colored and least processed tea contains the smallest amount of caffeine.

But Melican points out that age is just one of more than half a dozen factors that determine caffeine concentration. For example, the leaves of *C. sinensis* var. *assamica* consistently have higher levels of caffeine than the leaves of *C. sinensis* var. *sinensis*. How the bush was planted is another factor. Starting the bush from a clonal cutting (a cutting from a mother plant) rather than from a seedling results in a higher concentration. The time of year the leaf is plucked matters as well. If it is plucked in the hot growing season, the concentration will be higher than if it is plucked during cooler temperatures. A heavy dose of nitrogen fertilizer and shading the bushes, both common practices in Japan, will also increase the caffeine level. Once the leaves have come into the processing factory, the wither time will affect how much caffeine they retain. Finally, the water temperature used for steeping and the steeping time determine how much caffeine is extracted from the leaves. Typically, the hotter the water and the longer the steep, the more caffeine in your cup.

What all of this adds up to is that all tea has caffeine in it. What it also means is that leaves plucked on the same day from bushes in the same vicinity and then processed into different kinds of tea will have close to the same amount of caffeine in them. If you are concerned about caffeine for medical or personal reasons, there are a few things you can do. You can use the same leaves over again for multiple infusions at a lower water temperature, you can blend herbs with your tea to reduce the amount of tea in your cup, or, if you drink iced tea, you can water it down. If you cannot consume any caffeine, you cannot drink tea, because even decaffeinated teas have some caffeine in them. Consider drinking tisanes instead.

THE BUZZ ABOUT HEALTH

After attending the Fifth International Scientific Symposium on Tea and Human Health, in Washington, DC, I got even more excited about my favorite beverage. Dr. Jeffery Blumberg, who is a professor at the Friedman School of Nutrition Science and Policy and the director of the Antioxidants Research Laboratory at the Jean Mayer USDA Human Nutrition Research Center on Aging at Tufts University chaired the symposium, as he had done in 2007 and 2002. I was fortunate to have met Dr. Blumberg in 2008, when he attended one of my events, and he has been a great help to me ever since whenever

I have questions about the scientific findings on tea. His passion for tea and the science behind it is evident when you speak with him, and that passion was on full display at the symposium.

Not only is tea one of the oldest beverages on the planet, but it is also apparently one of the most researched. While attending the 2012 symposium on tea and human health, I listened to Dr. Blumberg's introductory lecture where he stated, "Many people aren't getting as many flavonoids as they need to in their diet. [One] way to get them is to drink tea. There is now an overwhelming body of research from around the world indicating that drinking tea can enhance human health. The many bioactive compounds in tea appear to impact virtually every cell in the body to help improve health outcomes, which is why the consensus emerging from this symposium is that drinking at least a cup of any class of tea a day can contribute significantly to the promotion of public health. If there's anything that can confidently be communicated to the public, it's the ability of tea to be associated and demonstrated in the primary prevention of chronic disease." Dr. Blumberg stresses that it is best to drink tea as a beverage rather than take supplements that contain the catechins or other compounds found in tea. When tea is steeped and imbibed, the thousands of bioactive elements present in tea leaves work together to affect almost every cell in the body, from the

Tea Research by the Numbers

From 2007 to 2012, more than 5,600 studies related to tea were produced: 2,878 on tea and general health, more than 1,000 on tea and cancer, more than 800 on tea and human health, more than 300 on black and green tea and weight loss, more than 100 on tea and heart health, 36 on tea and bone health, and 4 on tea and microbiome.

heart to the bones to the brain and even to the skin and gastrointestinal tract.

Even before the symposium, the data had been piling up on how good it is for you to drink tea on a daily basis. In 2011 alone, more than five hundred research papers were published on the subject of tea and various aspects of human health, and in just the first nine months of 2012, more than four hundred papers were published. The studies presented at the symposium focused on cardiovascular disease, cancer, cognitive improvements, osteoporosis, weight management, and a new interest, the possible probiotic effects of tea.

The research presented on heart health was promising, especially as related to blood pressure and stroke. Black tea appears to counteract the negative effect of a high-fat meal on blood pressure and arterial blood

flow. Dr. Claudio Ferri, of the University of L'Aquila in Italy, observed that, "Our studies build on previous work to clearly show that drinking as little as one cup of tea per day supports healthy arterial function and blood pressure. These results suggest that on a population scale, drinking tea could help reduce significantly the incidence of stroke, heart attack, and other cardiovascular diseases."

Flavonoids in the diet have been found to be effective in cancer prevention, as has caffeine, though to a lesser degree. Because tea contains both flavonoids and caffeine, it may play a role in helping to prevent cells from becoming cancerous. The initial findings presented at the symposium also suggest that tea may enhance the positive effects of the chemotherapy drugs used to treat some cancers, though more research is needed in both of these areas.

Most of us would agree that we can use a little boost in order to think and focus better. Tea appears to help us do both. When we are tired, caffeinated beverages of all kinds seem to perk us up. But the powerful combination of caffeine and L-theanine is found only in tea. Some observers call this dynamic pairing the yin and yang of the beverage, because it both alerts and calms the drinker. The most recent work supports past studies that found it also appears to help people focus better on the task at hand, heighten their creative problem-solving abilities, and improve their mood. So if you have a big project at work or a test coming up, drinking tea is definitely a good idea.

What about weight loss? Not surprisingly, the answer is not as simple as some advertisements would have you believe. The great news is that tea is calorie-free. Because the calories consumed by drinking various other beverages throughout the day can add up quickly, tea is a great choice. It also reportedly hydrates the body as effectively as water but with the added benefit of antioxidants. Science shows that drinking tea may assist in promoting weight loss. The mixture of caffeine and catechins seems not only to increase a person's energy expenditure but also helps modestly with fat oxidation, which means it's burning fat, too. Be careful, however, as drinking tea can also increase your appetite, so it matters what you eat while you are drinking it.

Osteoporosis is a serious problem as we age. So far there is no a cure for it, but preventative measures do seem to delay its onset. The studies on tea and osteoporosis are few, but the results are encouraging. Combining some type of weight-bearing exercise, such as tai chi, with drinking tea has been shown to help decrease inflammation and increase bone density and muscle strength, thereby protecting against the onset of osteoporosis.

The final topic of the symposium, the probiotic effect of tea drinking, was new to most of the attendees, and although only minimal research has been completed, the findings warrant more studies in the future. Some flavonoids in tea are digested and absorbed, but others seem to be resistant to digestion. Those that are not digested travel down to the lower gastrointestinal tract, where they appear to provide a probiotic effect by enabling beneficial bacteria to thrive. So when you don't feel well, the advice to drink tea may not be an old wives' tale after all. Science is beginning to back up what your grandmother told you to do. This probiotic effect may even help ward off the illness before it settles in.

Other studies presented looked at how tea aids oral health, decreases inflammation, and works toward a healthy immune system. All of the new data taken together, along with past research, points to the benefits of drinking tea.

So what class of tea should you drink for good health? Remember, drinking tea should be pleasurable not only for how it tastes but also for how it makes you feel. And although it is not a medicine, it can be part of a healthy lifestyle. That means that the best teas to consume for your health are the ones that you love to drink, because if you love the tea, you will naturally drink more of it. And because all tea is good for you, the health benefits that come with drinking the tea you love are just an especially nice bonus.

THE BUZZ ABOUT CHOOSING COFFEE OR TEA

There doesn't need to be a battle when it comes to deciding between being a coffee person and a tea person. I think you can be both, and many people are. Nobody says that you cannot drink beer if you drink wine, or that you cannot enjoy bourbon if you like tequila. Indeed, it is silly to think that you have to choose one over the other. In fact, I was once quite passionate about drinking coffee, but over the last decade or so, coffee proved not to be passionate about me! It began to bother my stomach, and I decided my zeal for the beverage was not greater than my desire to feel good. So I stopped drinking it. I still enjoy a sip from time to time, and I am absolutely crazy for the smell, but I know that I should not drink it often, and when I do, I should stop at a few sips.

For a variety of reasons, a lot of folks have had to give up coffee. Many coffee lovers have asked me how they can begin incorporating more tea into their daily life. For some it is a matter of health. They have heard the news about the health benefits of tea and want to begin drinking it. Or, they have been told by their doctor to stop drinking their coffee because of a medical condition.

Others are like me and have found that their bodies will no longer tolerate coffee for some unexplained reason. Still others want to cut back on their caffeine intake because of how it makes them feel. A cup of tea has less caffeine than a cup of coffee on average, but because tea contains both caffeine along with two other methylxanthines that act as stimulants and muscle relaxants and L-theanine, you naturally feel differently when drinking it. Most people say that tea gives them a smooth, sustained level of alertness, rather than the instant buzz and quick drop-off that coffee delivers.

Because coffee is much different from tea in more than taste, it is difficult for the hardcore coffee drinker to make the switch. Discovering the right tea for a coffee person boils down to trying to figure out what that person likes about his or her coffee and then finding a tea that shares similarities, even though the match won't fit every characteristic. If you are a coffee drinker and want to add tea to your regular regimen or you want to switch to tea, here are some suggestions.

If the aroma of coffee is what drives you to drink it, you may be drawn to a black Chinese Keemun. I find the aroma is similar though not as pungent as coffee. Another option is a black Chinese Yunnan. To me, its aroma has the richness, plus some chocolaty notes.

If you like coffee because it is robust and bold, you need a tea with the same qualities. A black tea such as an Indian Assam, a low-grown Ceylon, a breakfast blend, or a Kenyan fits that description. If you take your coffee with cream or milk and sugar and cannot imagine giving them up, these same black teas should work for you. In fact, all of these teas are often drunk with cream or milk and/or sugar in their country of origin and elsewhere around the globe. Masala Chai, also known as chai tea (mistakenly, as *chai* means "tea" in Hindi) or sometimes chai latte, is another popular tea-and-milk combo. A blend of black tea and spices that originated in India, it is traditionally mixed with hot milk and sugar. (Cream will sometimes curdle when you add it to black tea because of the high temperature of the steeping water, so you may want to switch to whole or reduced-fat milk. But if you enjoy the taste of cream and tea and a little curdling doesn't bother you, go ahead and add it.)

If you like the effects of caffeine, look to teas that are known to have more caffeine in them. As explained earlier in this chapter, teas made from *C. sinensis* var. *assamica* typically have higher caffeine levels, which means that the same robust and bold black teas just listed would be good choices. Drinking a green tea or a white tea is a bit of a stretch for serious coffee drinkers, but some teas in these classes are also known to be high in caffeine. For a morning or afternoon

Tea Has More and Less Caffeine Than Coffee

How can that be? Based on dry weight, 1 lb/455 g of tea contains about twice the amount of caffeine as an equal amount of coffee. But 1 lb/455 g of coffee yields between fifty and sixty cups of brewed coffee and the same amount of tea will yield about two hundred cups.

A 1997 study that appeared in *Critical Reviews in Plant Sciences* found that a 6-oz/170-ml cup of tea averages about 45 mg of caffeine, while the same amount of coffee averages about 97.5 mg. On closer examination, however, the range of caffeine is broad for both. According to the study, coffee ranges between 40 and 155 mg caffeine per 6-oz/170-ml serving and tea ranges between 20 and 70 mg. That means that on average in the weight arena, tea wins the caffeine race, but cup for cup, coffee is the winner.

boost, try a shade-grown Japanese green tea such as Matcha or Gyokuro. If you are a bit more daring, experiment with a Silver Needle white tea, which is known to deliver a caffeine jolt. It won't give you the bold flavor of coffee, but its subtle sweet flavor may be just what your body needs.

If you are longing for a medium-roasted, nutty flavor, steep a pot of Japanese green Hojicha, which undergoes a roasting step after processing that gives it a toasty taste. Another Japanese green option is Genmaicha, tea mixed with toasted brown rice that imparts a warm roasted taste when steeped. Or you might like one of the baked oolongs, such as an amber oolong, which spends time in a low oven after processing, where it takes on a lovely baked aroma and taste.

If you like a dark roast coffee, such as French or Italian, you might enjoy a lightly smoky Chinese black tea such as Keemun or a deeply smoky Chinese black such as Lapsong Souchong. Both teas tend toward an aggressive flavor profile, with a "manly" appeal. Folks who like Scotch typically like these teas, too. If you like the malty taste in beer, then a malty Assam black tea might do the trick. Yet another option on an entirely different spectrum of flavor is a dark tea, such as a Pu'erh. It can be smooth and earthy, especially if it is a well-aged Sheng Pu'erh.

Keep in mind that if you decide to switch, the lifestyle of tea is much different from that of coffee. While coffee is considered fast-paced, tea is a slower beverage, both because of how it is brewed and how it is digested in your body. In other words, you will not only be making an adjustment in flavor but also decelerating your life a bit. This might be just what the doctor ordered.

THE BUZZ ABOUT SUSTAINABILITY

For most of us living in the West, buying locally grown specialty tea isn't an option, so we must rely on our community retail stores or Internet suppliers for our knowledge about their tea sources. I like to shop with what I call a "local global" approach. In other words, I regularly seek information about the international teas I am buying from the staff where I buy my teas. Tea purveyors should know where their teas are sourced and the farming methods used to grow them. If these things matter to you, show it not just by asking the necessary questions but also by paying more for teas that meet your standards.

Tea is a highly sustainable crop. *C. sinensis* bushes can typically survive under good conditions for a hundred years or more. In China, tea bushes several centuries old are still yielding a harvest. Fortunately, *C. sinensis* does not have many natural predators, either. Nowadays, research centers around the world are developing new cultivars that will withstand wider variations in the environment, ensuring an even more sustainable crop. These newly introduced plants also have the potential to produce a greater output and a greater resistance to harmful pests.

Bigger harvests and fewer chemicals are good for the farmer, the soil, and the consumer.

I have visited several tea plantations, estates, and gardens where sustainable and ethical practices had been or were being implemented. It was inspiring to see forests being preserved, computer and English classes being taught to the workers to help them better themselves and their children, clean hospitals offering free care for workers and their families, and organic farming methods in effect that benefited the environment and the tea. A number of buzz words are used to describe these sustainable tea operations, and to be an educated shopper, you need to understand them in order to choose the best tea for you. Here are explanations for the six most commonly encountered terms.

Organic Farming

Many believe that seeking out organic products whenever possible is important for both our health and our environment. Each country has its own list of criteria for something to be labeled *organic*, but here are the most common inclusions for growing conditions: no chemicals, antibiotics, synthetic hormones, genetic modification, or use of sewage sludge as fertilizer. In addition, the finished product cannot contain artificial ingredients or preservatives or have undergone irradiation.

Organic certification begins at the source with a third-party agency. These agencies have been approved by inspectors of the country to which the tea will be shipped. Once the agency verifies that the tea complies with the established standards, it can be exported. These approved agencies are trusted to do the necessary paperwork that will follow the tea all the way to the wholesaler. This transparent paper trail is one of the most important factors in ensuring that the tea is certified organic. In the United States, the United States Department of Agriculture (USDA) follows practices enacted by the National Organic Program (NOP), and in Canada, the Canadian Food Inspection Agency (CFIA) observes rules established by the Canada Organic Regime (COR). The European Union (EU) likewise has its own set of strict guidelines for its members.

The wholesaler who will distribute the tea must also be certified by a third-party agency. An audit is done onsite to ensure that good record keeping showing full transparency has been carried out from the farm to the wholesale facility. For a product to display the USDA Organic seal in the United States, the CFIA Canada Organic Biologique logo in Canada, or the seal of the EU logo in its member states, 95 percent of its ingredients must be organic. Some products labeled "organic" may not have complied with all of the regulations required along the purchasing chain. So, if you are seeking an organic product, check the necessary certifications carefully.

One Small Organization with a Big Organic Mission

When I was in Taiwan in 2010 traveling with a group led by Thomas Shu of ABC Teas, we were the first international visitors to be invited to visit a wonderful Buddhist community in the picturesque Pinglin area, located high in the mountains near Taipei. As we arrived, the community greeted us with smiles and sang and clapped. Their mission is to promote religion, culture, and charity, which they do through the nonprofit Tse-Xin Organic Agriculture Foundation.

Tse-Xin, which means "mercy heart," lives up to its name. When it was discovered that the Feicui Reservoir that supplies water for some seven million people in the Taipei metropolitan area was being polluted by the runoff of chemicals and pesticides, the community organized the Pure Spring Reservoir Protecting Project. Their primary focus was to teach the tea growers, who are the main farmers in the area, how to work their land organically. This in turn would ensure both clean, safe drinking water for everyone who draws water from the reservoir and organic tea. The training needed to reach every corner of the area, so that the farms converting to organic practices on the lower part of the mountain would not get the runoff of nonorganic substances from farms higher up the mountain.

Helped by donations from private sources and the government and guidance from the Taiwan Tea Research and Extension Station (TRES), the members of Tse-Xin are slowly making a difference. They know that it is challenging to convince farmers to change their ways, and they support them through various programs. For example, they instruct them in how to use organic fertilizers in place of synthetic fertilizers. They also show them how spreading peanut shells between the plant rows is good for two reasons: the shells cut down on weeds and provide the soil with much-needed nitrogen. One of the greatest challenges is dealing with the loss of production for about three years as the plants get used to the new regimen. This downtime can take an enormous financial toll on farm families. In response, Tse-Xin provides free liquid organic fertilizer and offers loans and monetary aid to those whose farms are in transition.

When it is harvesttime, the farmers can utilize the foundation's organic factory to process their tea. There are no worries about the price or the sale of the tea when it is ready. The foundation and the farmer have set the price together, and the foundation agrees to purchase all of the tea!

So, why not always buy organic tea? Some countries or regions do not have organic certification programs in place yet, though that does not always mean that the farmers are not practicing organic methods. Long before there were pesticides, tea was being grown and consumed, and some farmers continue to cultivate tea the way their ancestors taught them. Also, using pesticides is not an option for some farmers due to lack of availability or cost. For others, this natural way of farming comes at a price they cannot afford: the cost of inspections and certification, of the materials needed to convert to organic methods, and of lost production as the fields acclimate to the change. Fortunately, as consumers begin to demand more organic products and show a willingness to pay higher prices for them, tea farmers at origin, knowing there is a market for organic tea, are more likely to begin to comply with the costly organic methods. In recent years, organic teas have become a steadily growing segment of the specialty tea market.

Biodynamic Farming

Biodynamic agriculture, which combines organic farming practices with a holistic approach to the soil, plants, and animals, originated with Rudolf Steiner in Germany in 1924. The basic premise is to treat the whole farm as a single working organism that marries nature and the cosmic rhythms of the sun, moon, planets, and stars to create a self-nourishing system in total ecological harmony.

A variety of herbal compost preparations and homeopathic field sprays are used to promote plant growth, ensure soil health, and control fungal and other diseases. For example, one of the most popular field sprays calls for filling a cow horn with a paste made of crushed quartz and water, burying the horn in the summer, and then digging it up in the fall. The paste is removed from the horn and diluted to make a fine slurry, which is sprayed on plants to encourage growth. Biodynamic farmers also irrigate crops with a close eye to water conservation and are required to set aside at least 10 percent of their total acreage as a riparian zone, wetland, grassland, or forest land, or all of these designations.

Certification for biodynamic farms is handled by Demeter International, which oversees the verification of biodynamic standards in more than fifty countries. The first tea farm to receive this distinction was the Makaibari Tea Estate, located in Darjeeling, in 1991. Fourth-generation tea owner Rajah Banerjee took over the garden from his father and began to practice farming in a completely different way after reading Rudolf Steiner's teachings. He was not only the first to convert a tea garden to biodynamic farming but also the first to be certified a fair trade operation (see page 155). His recognition does not stop there, however. Banerjee has led the charge to promote women to supervisory positions.

At this time, biodynamic tea farms are rare and are growing at a slow rate. But with the prices that Makaibari tea continues to command, the message of change is slowly increasing.

Ozone-Friendly Farming

This is a rather new term in the tea world, and to date, Sri Lanka's tea farmers are the only ones using it. The 1987 Montreal Protocol agreement was ratified by 196 countries to gradually reduce and eventually eliminate the use of the pesticide known as methyl bromide (MB). Although MB was effective in eliminating harmful insects, worms, and weeds that attack cropland, it was found to be a danger to the ozone layer. Sri Lanka responded to the protocol by beginning an aggressive total phaseout of the product. In 2007, Canada gave Sri Lanka the Montreal Protocol Implementers Award for achieving ozone-friendly tea status.

Rainforest Alliance

The Rainforest Alliance, a nongovernmental organization founded in New York City in 1986, strives to maintain biodiversity, encourage sustainable land use, and improve the lives of workers in countries around the world. Toward those ends, it has established sustainable forestry and agricultural certification programs, among others. I have been lucky to visit tea plantations in Sri Lanka that have been certified by the alliance, including the New Vithanakande Estate (see page 19, "What Is Specialty Tea?"), a well-known source of low-grown tea that was undergoing the certification process at the time of my visit and has subsequently received it. I also stayed overnight on Dessford Estate, located high in the Dimbula Valley in central Sri Lanka. Its tea fields are at around 5,000 ft/1,500 m and are surrounded by abundant forests and mountains. Both of these operations and many others like them face a constant battle on how best to balance forest preservation with the need for firewood to power their factories.

Rainforest Alliance also promotes such children's initiatives as education and health care and works to increase workers' wages, reduce chemicals in the soil, and encourage water management. Farms trying to obtain Rainforest Alliance certification must meet at least 80 percent of the standard criteria for their crop as established by the Sustainable Agriculture Network (SAN), which oversees the certification practices. Once the farms have been certified, annual audits are held to ensure there is no slippage and required improvements are continuing to be made. By working along the supply chain from the field to the buyer, Rainforest

Alliance hopes to create a healthy collaboration that ensures a better way of doing business. As of 2012, 10 percent of the global tea market was Rainforest Alliance certified.

Fair Trade

The fair trade movement, which focuses on certifying a variety of products in underdeveloped countries, helps producers secure a fair price for their product, fair wages and safe working conditions for their workers, direct trade with buyers, and environmental sustainability, among other benefits. The earliest attempts to promote fair trade products date back to the 1940s, and by the 1960s, the movement was well established in Europe. Today, most countries, though certainly not all, rely on Fairtrade International, which labeled its first product in 1988, to oversee standards and certification. The United States, which split from the group in September 2011, uses Fair Trade USA for its mark. The primary fallout of this split is that the change in labeling has confused some buyers in the United States.

Of course, a number of tea-producing countries that enjoy good labor conditions and practice environmental sustainability will never fall under the fair trade banner. In other words, you won't see a fair trade label on a Taiwanese or Japanese tea. But finding the label does not always ensure quality, either, as some companies have been known to use it as a marketing ploy without following through on the tenets of the movement. There are also concerns about how much of the extra money paid to the brokers selling fair trade tea actually reaches the farmers and workers. If fair trade practices are important to you, ask your tea purveyors if they have fully explored whether the fair trade teas they sell are products of a successful program.

Ethical Tea Partnership

The Ethical Tea Partnership (ETP) was formed in 1997 with the vision that large international brands and smaller independent labels could work together for a more socially and environmentally sustainable industry. It is made up of more than twenty members from Europe, North America, Australia, and New Zealand representing more than fifty brands sold in more than one hundred countries.

Through collaborative agreements with other organizations such as the Rainforest Alliance and Fairtrade International, the members help producers improve the training, health, safety, and wages of their workers and achieve certification. They also assist producers in adapting to climate change and other environmental issues, increasing energy efficiency, and securing access to markets.

RESOURCES

I encourage you to find a tea shop in your area and to develop a rapport with the staff. But if there is no tea shop where you live, this guide suggests reputable online resources for buying tea, teaware, and tea equipment.

Tea and Tea Accessories

North America

Adagio
www.adagio.com
A notable selection of specialty teas, including flavored and scented teas, and a plentiful array of teapots, teacups, kettles, and tea accessories. Also carries cupping sets. Retail locations in the Chicago area.

Davids Tea
www.davidstea.com
Known for its interesting inventory of flavored specialty teas. Good selection of mostly contemporary teapots and teacups. Also carries a wide variety of travel mugs and infusers. Retail shops in Canada and the United States.

Den's Tea
www.denstea.com
Specializes in Japanese teas and teapots, teacups, and accessories.

Rishi Tea
www.rishi-tea.com
Sources fair trade and organic teas whenever possible. Ample selection of fine teas along with a limited array of high-quality flavored teas. Teapots and teacups are modern and mainly Eastern-style.

SerendipiTea
www.serendipitea.com
One of the early specialty tea companies in North America. Sources organic, biodynamic, and fair trade teas whenever possible. Fine selection of flavored teas along with an excellent variety of botanicals, herbs, and spices.

Silk Road Tea
www.silkroadteastore.com
Tea store and spa located in Victoria, Canada. The online store has a lovely selection of organic teas, teaware, and private-label skin, bath, and body products that are locally made using all natural ingredients. This is wonderful if, like me, you are sensitive to artificial fragrances. You can even create your own spa products by mixing the company's essential oils with its unscented shampoo, bath salts, and soaps.

Teaism
www.teaism.com
Good selection of specialty teas and unique pottery items available online. Teahouse restaurants feature tea in their recipes, along with vegetarian, vegan, and gluten-free options. Four locations in the Washington, D.C., area.

TeaSource
www.teasource.com
One of the early specialty tea companies in North America. Excellent online selection of teas (especially dark teas), teapots of all kinds, and a wonderful array of tea accessories, including Chinese tea ceremony smelling cups, scales, and instant-read thermometers. Retail locations in the St. Paul, Minnesota, area.

Teas Etc
www.teasetc.com
Specializes in organic teas and other quality tea selections. Nice selection of herbal tisane blends.

United Kingdom

Postcard Teas

www.postcardteas.com
Excellent selection of teas from around the world. The site also features a wide assortment of Eastern-style teapots and cups. Retail location in London.

Teapod

www.teapodtea.co.uk
Limited but good selection of specialty teas online. Retail locations in London are contemporary teahouses.

France

Mariage Frères

www.mariagefreres.com
Abundant selection of fine teas; known especially for its flavored teas. It also carries unique teapots and tea accoutrements. Retail locations in Paris and other French cities, in London, in Germany, and in Japan, some with salons, museums, and restaurants.

Le Palais des Thés

www.palaisdesthes.com
Grand assortment of fine teas from all over the world and lovely selection of teaware. Retail locations in France, Ireland, Belgium, Norway, Slovenia, Japan, Israel, and the United States. The Paris, France, location offers a wide variety of educational classes and trips to origin for hands-on learning.

Electric Kettles and Water Heaters

If you are going to start investing in tea equipment, upgrading to an electric kettle with an adjustable thermostat is a great place to start. Another option is an electric water heater that not only heats the water but also holds the selected temperature for an extended time.

Breville

www.brevilleusa.com

Cuisinart

www.cuisinart.com

Edgecraft Chef's Choice

www.chefschoice.com

Zojirushi

www.zojirushi.com

Tea Associations and Trade Show

The Tea Association of the USA

www.teausa.com
www.teausa.org

Tea Association of Canada

www.tea.ca

United Kingdom Tea Council

www.tea.co.uk

World Tea Media

www.worldteaexpo.com
The first and only tea trade show and conference. It is a great place to get started in the tea business and to continue learning, with opportunities for tea-focused seminars, business education, tea tastings, and networking. Open to the trade only.

SELECT BIBLIOGRAPHY

Books

Banerjee, Rajah. *The Rajah of Darjeeling Organic Tea: Makaibari*. Delhi: Cambridge University Press India Pvt. Ltd., 2008.

Compestine, Ying Chang. *Cooking with Green Tea*. New York: Avery, 2000.

Dornenburg, Andrew, and Karen Page. *What to Drink with What You Eat: The Definitive Guide to Pairing Food with Wine, Beer, Spirits, Coffee, Tea—Even Water—Based on Expert Advice from America's Best Sommeliers*. New York: Bulfinch, 2006.

Eskin, N. A. Michael, and Snait Tamir. *Dictionary of Nutraceuticals and Functional Foods*. Boca Raton, FL: Taylor & Francis Group/CRC Press, 2006.

Fellman, Donna, and Lhasha Tizer. *Tea Here Now: Rituals, Remedies, and Meditations*. Makawao, Maui, HI: Inner Ocean, 2005.

Jakuan, Sotaku. *The Book of Zen Tea*. 1828.

Joly, Nicolas. *Biodynamic Wine, Demystified*. San Francisco: Wine Appreciation Guild, 2008.

Lefcourte, Atsuko Y. *Life with Tea*. New York: Muse, 1998.

Morikami Museum and Japanese Gardens. *The Tea Ceremony*. Delray, FL: Morikami Museum and Japanese Gardens, n.d.

Okakura, Kakuzo. *The Book of Tea*. Rutland, VT: C. E. Tuttle, 1956.

Parr, Rajat, Jordan Mackay, and Ed Anderson. *Secrets of the Sommeliers: How to Think and Drink Like the World's Top Wine Professionals*. Berkeley, CA: Ten Speed Press, 2010.

Pettigrew, Jane. *A Social History of Tea*. London: National Trust, 2001.

Sen XV, Sōshitsu. "Tea in the Heian Era." Chap. 3 in *The Japanese Way of Tea: From Its Origins in China to Sen Rikyū*. Translated by V. Dixon Morris. Honolulu: University of Hawaii Press, 1998.

Willson, K. C., and M. N. Clifford. *Tea: Cultivation to Consumption*. London: Springer, 1992.

Articles

Arab, Lenore, and Jeffrey B. Blumberg. "Introduction to the Proceedings of the Fourth International Scientific Symposium on Tea and Human Health." *The Journal of Nutrition* 138, no. 8 (2008) 1526s-1528s.

Chin, Jenna M., Michele L. Merves, Bruce A. Goldberger, Angela Sampson-Cone, and Edward J. Cone. "Caffeine Content of Brewed Teas." *Journal of Analytical Toxicology* 32, no. 8 (October 2008): 702–704. doi:10.1093/jat/32.8.702.

Enticott, Richard. "The Truth about Decaffeinated Tea." *Tea Experience Digest* (Spring 2007): 33–42.

Harbowy, M. E., and D. A. Balentine. "Tea Chemistry." *Critical Reviews in Plant Sciences* 16, no. 5 (1997): 415–80.

Hilal, Y., and U. Engelhardt. "Characterisation of White Tea—Comparison to Green and Black Tea." *Journal Für Verbraucherschutz Und Lebensmittelsicherheit* 2, no. 4 (2007): 414–21.

Richardson, Bruce. "Debunking the Myth of Tea's Caffeine Content." *Fresh Cup* (January 2009): 52–54.

Media

Jones, Stephen R. "'How to Do Tips' for Wu-Wo Tea Ceremony." Tea Arts (blog). teaarts.blogspot.com/2007/02/1st-wu-wo-tea-ceremony-fallbrook-ca.html.

Melican, Nigel. "Caffeine and Tea: Myth and Reality." Cha Dao (blog). chadao.blogspot.com/2008/02/caffeine-and-tea-myth-and-reality.html.

Robertson, Dan. *The Art of Chinese Tea: The Tea Ceremony*. DVD. Directed by Bob Abrant and Dan Robertson. Naperville, IL: The Tea House, 2005.

"Why Wine and Tea Pair so Well with a Meal: It's All in the Mouthfeel." *e! Science News*, October 8, 2012. www.sciencedaily.com/releases/2012/10/121008134215.htm.

INDEX

A

Afternoon tea, 99, 101–2, 103
Antioxidants, 139, 140
Assam, 41

B

Bagua Tea Garden, 17
Bai Hao, 37, 38
Bancha, 32
Baozhong, 37, 38
Beauty products, tea in, 132
Big Red Robe, 37, 38
Biodynamic farming, 153–54
Black tea, 41–44, 64

C

Caffeine, 142–45, 148, 149
Catechins, 140–41, 145, 147
Catherine of Braganza, 16, 99
Ceylon teas, 16, 20–21, 41, 42–43
Chado, 90
Chanoyu, 90–93, 95–96
Charles II (king of England), 16, 99
Charleston Tea Plantation, 15, 18
China
    black teas of, 44
    dark teas of, 44, 46
    green teas of, 28, 30
    oolong teas of, 37
    tea ceremony in, 83, 85–86, 88–90
    tea cultivation in, 13, 15
    white teas of, 26, 28
    yellow teas of, 35
Cocktails, 128, 130–31
Coffee vs. tea, 148–50
Cooking with tea, 123–25, 127–28
Cupping, 43, 79

D

Da Hong Pao, 37, 38
Darjeeling tea, 20, 41, 44, 64
Dark tea, 44, 46, 57, 64
Decaffeination, 143
Delmas, François-Xavier, 119
Dong Ding. See Tung Ting
Dragon Well, 30

E

EGCG (epigallocatechin gallate), 140, 141
England
    history of tea in, 16, 99
    tea ceremonies in, 99, 101–3
    tea cultivation in, 18–19
Ethical Tea Partnership, 155

F

Fair trade movement, 155
Flavonoids, 140–41, 145, 146, 147
Flavored teas, 52
Food, pairing tea and, 118–20, 122–23
France, tea drinking in, 106–7
Franks, Melanie, 124
Free radicals, 140

G

Gardening, 134
Genmaicha, 32
Gentleman Mountain Silver Needles, 35
Gold, Cynthia, 123
Gongfu cha, 83, 85–86, 88–90
Green tea
    in beauty products, 132
    Chinese, 28, 30
    Japanese, 30, 32
    oxidation and, 28
    steeping times for, 64
Gunpowder, 30
Gustafson, Helen, 115
Gyokuro, 32

H

Health, 131–32, 139–42, 145–47
Herbal infusions, 14, 64
High tea, 102–3
Hojicha, 32
Huangshan Maofeng, 30
Huo Mountain Yellow Sprout, 35

I

Iced tea, 67–68
India
    black teas of, 41, 44
    tea cultivation in, 16
Infusers, 58
Iran, tea drinking in, 110
Iron Goddess of Mercy. *See* Tie Guanyin

J

Japan
    green teas of, 30, 32
    tea ceremony in, 90–93, 95–96
    tea cultivation in, 15, 31

K

Kassab, Karl, 117
Keemun, 44
Kenya, tea cultivation in, 16
Kettles, 58
Kotiyagala Estate, 42–43
Kukicha, 32

L

Labe, James, 116, 122
Longjing, 30
Lover's Leap tea, 21

M

Matcha, 32, 55, 57, 95
Meditation, 110–11
Mengding Yellow Sprout, 35
Moroccan tea ceremony, 104, 106
Mount Jun Yellow Tip, 35

N

New Vithanakande Estate, 20, 154
Nhat Hanh, Thich, 110–11
Nicholson, Jim, 116
Nischan, Michel, 116

O

Oolong tea, 37–39, 64
Organic tea, 151–53
Oriental Beauty, 37, 38
Orthodox production, 22, 141
Oxidation, 25, 26, 28, 44, 140–41
Ozone-friendly farming, 154

P

Pedro Estate, 21
Pi (Bi) Luo Chun, 30
Polyphenols, 140
Pouchong, 37, 38
Pu'erh, 44, 46

R

Rainforest Alliance, 154–55
Rikyu, Sen no, 90, 91
Russia, tea drinking in, 107, 109

S

Samovars, 107, 109, 110
Scented teas, 52
Sencha, 32
Sheng Pu'erh, 46
Shennong, 13
Shizuoka Cha Ichiba, 31
Shou Mei, 28
Shou Pu'erh, 46
Silver Needle, 28, 144
Silver Tip, 37, 38
Smell, sense of, 69–70, 73
Smelling cups, 86

Smoking with tea, 127–28
Sri Lanka. *See* Ceylon teas
Steeping
    Eastern style, 61
    equipment for, 58
    times for, 64
    water for, 57–58, 62, 64–65
    Western style, 61–62, 64
Sustainability, 150–55

T

Taiwan
    oolong teas of, 37, 38, 39
    tea ceremony in, 96–98
    tea cultivation in, 16, 17
Tasting, 51, 68–70, 72–79
Tea
    in beauty products, 132
    black, 41–44, 64
    blends of, 21
    botanical classification of, 13–14
    buying, 51–52, 54–55
    caffeine in, 142–45, 148, 149
    classes of, 13, 15, 26
    in cocktails, 128, 130–31
    coffee vs., 148–50
    cooking with, 123–25, 127–28
    cultivars of, 14
    dark, 44, 46, 57, 64
    decaffeinated, 143
    flavored, 52
    in gardens, 134
    geographical distribution of, 15–19
    green, 28, 30, 32, 64

growing, 14, 15–19

health and, 131–32, 139–42, 145–47

history of, 13, 15–16, 18–19, 22, 41

iced, 67–68

oolong, 37–39, 64

other uses for, 134–35

pairing food and, 118–20, 122–23

plucking, 22, 25

popularity of, 9

production of, 21–22, 24–26, 141

scented, 52

smoking with, 127–28

specialty, 19–21, 50

steeping, 57–58, 61–62, 64–65

storing, 55, 57

sustainability and, 150–55

tasting, 51, 68–70, 72–79

white, 26, 28, 64

yellow, 35, 64

Tea ceremonies and rituals

    Chinese, 83, 85–86, 88–90

    English, 99, 101–3

    French, 106–7

    Iranian, 110

    Japanese, 90–93, 95–96

    meditation and, 110–11

    Moroccan, 104, 106

    Russian, 107, 109

    Taiwanese, 96–98

Teapots, 58

Tea sommeliers, 115–18

Tea tins, empty, 135

Terroir, 19–20

Theanine, 141–42, 146, 148

Theobromine, 142

Theophylline, 142

Tie Guanyin, 38

Tregothnan Estate, 18–19

Tse-Xin Organic Agriculture Foundation, 152

Tung Ting, 37, 38, 39

U

United States, tea cultivation in, 15, 16, 18

Usucha, 92–93

W

Wang Ting Tea Garden, 17

Water

    boiling, 62

    flavor of, 57–58

    importance of, 57

    temperature of, 64–65

White Peony, 28

White Silver Tip, 37, 38

White tea, 26, 28, 64

Wu-wo, 96–98

Y

Yellow tea, 35, 64

Yunnan, 44

Z

Zhu Cha, 30

ACKNOWLEDGMENTS

I am deeply grateful to my tea mentors, friends, and colleagues who have been extremely helpful as I have researched this book. Your knowledge and opinions have meant a great deal to me. This group includes Dr. Jeffrey Blumberg, director of the Antioxidants Research Laboratory at Tufts University; Donna Fellman of World Tea Media; Suzette Hammond of Rishi Tea; Elliot Jordan of Peet's Coffee & Tea; Judith Krall-Russo; Nigel Melican of Tea Craft; Thomas Shu of ABC Tea; Mike Spillane of G.S. Haly Company; Linda Villano of SerendipiTea; Bill Waddington of TeaSource; and David Walker of Walker Tea.

A special thank-you goes to my agent Lisa Ekus and the staff at the Lisa Ekus Group. It has been a pleasure working with all of you on this project. Also, I am deeply appreciative to coffee-loving Editorial Director Bill LeBlond at Chronicle Books for his vision and the opportunity to write this book on tea. It is an honor to be included among the many talented authors he has worked with in the past. I would also like to thank Amy Treadwell at Chronicle Books for her thoughtful suggestions, hard work, and editing on the book and to Sharon Silva for all her insightful edits to the manuscript.

It was wonderful to work with Jen Altman on the photography. Her photos brought my words to life and show the reader the visual beauty of tea. I also want to thank Bill Waddington of TeaSource *again* for sponsoring all the tea used in the photos for the book. I'm also appreciative of those companies that allowed us to borrow their beautiful products to use as props for the photo shoot on this project: For Life Design, Silk Road Tea, Tavalon Tea, and TeaSource.

Finally, I am so blessed to have a husband and kids who support their passionate tea-geek wife and mom as I pursue my dreams. Thanks, Joe, for all your love and the hours you have spent reading and editing my work, listening to me talk about tea, and sipping tea with me. I look forward to drinking tea with you for the rest of our lives!

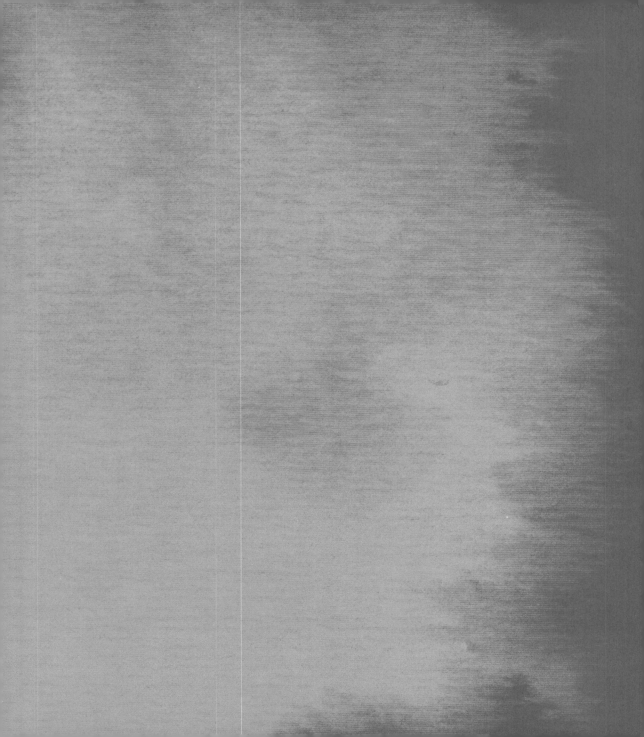